10

FINANCIAL STRATEGIES
FOR THE SMART INVESTOR

10

FINANCIAL STRATEGIES
FOR THE SMART INVESTOR

HOW TO AVOID COMMON MISTAKES
AND BUILD LASTING WEALTH

MARK CHANDIK

Printed in the United States of America

ISBN Paperback: 9780692596876
ISBN Hardcover: 9780692596869
ISBN eBook: 978-0-692-59688-3

Library of Congress Control Number: 2015920584

Cover design: Michelle Manley
Interior design: Ghislain Viau

To my loving wife and best friend, Cindy.
Our 31 years together continue to be my source for
motivation, encouragement, and humbleness.

To my daughters, Caitlin and Madeline, who
sometimes take my advice but always provide
me with unconditional love and joy.

Contents

Acknowledgments

To my parents, Richard and Flo. Thank you for raising me to be independent and encouraging me to always strive to be better each and every day.

To my business partner, Bryan Ugalde. You are many things to me: friend, coworker, partner, brother, and son—all wrapped in one. It has been a joy to collaborate with you over the past thirteen years.

To my longtime friend and business partner, Larry Lee, you have provided endless advice on marriage, raising children, and being a humble human being. I will be forever grateful.

To my weekend coffee buddies, Dave, Dave, and Pat. You have all been a sounding board for me over the years through good times and bad. We have shared each other's triumphs and challenges, but in the end, we have shared the gift of a deep and loving friendship.

To all who helped me put this book together, especially Andy Wolfendon and Sara Stratton. You kept me on task and focused. The process reinforced my belief that a result is always better when people work in collaboration.

To the countless clients and fellow professionals with whom I have had the honor to work over the years. Thank you for giving me the opportunity to serve you and, most of all, to build a long-term, meaningful relationship with you. I have benefited through the sharing of your family histories, successes, and failures. I am truly blessed and humbled by the trust you have placed in me.

Introduction

Money affects everything. From our basic survival needs to our loftiest goals and dreams, no aspect of human life is untouched by money. Money may not buy happiness, but it goes a long way toward determining the make and model of happiness we end up pursuing.

And yet most of us know very little about money for one simple reason: We haven't been taught. In grammar school and high school all we really learned was how to make change for a twenty and balance a checkbook. Maybe we took an economics course in college, but that knowledge is safely tucked away in the dark halls of our minds, along with Aristotle's *Poetics* and the Hundred Years' War.

Isn't it strange that something so essential to human life—something we crave, celebrate, kill for, die for, fight

1

over, identify with, obsess about, and work our whole lives to acquire—is left largely unexplained?

But that's the startling truth. And so most of us are forced to create our own financial education on the fly. We borrow a little bit from over here, a little bit from over there. We pick up pieces from our parents, our peers, and the media. Most of what we absorb is based on other people's experiences—their fears and hopes and desires. If our parents or grandparents lived through the Great Depression, for example, we probably learned that the stock market is evil.

By the time we're in our twenties, most of us have stitched together the basic money beliefs that will carry us through adulthood. And many, if not most, of these beliefs are pure fantasy. Often they're not even consistent with one another. They are based on emotion, not logic or fact.

I've been a wealth manager for over thirty years and I've had the good fortune of working with thousands of people—and their money. Over those years I've been able to observe two distinct kinds of individual: those who easily succeed at the money game and those who just can't seem to make it work. And what I've learned is that the successful people consistently do certain things right. They embrace certain beliefs, principles, and behaviors—and they stick with them through good economic times and bad, through all of life's dramas and challenges.

The others? They cling to illusions and repeat mistakes. *Predictable* mistakes. In my practice I've come to recognize that people make the same common handful of money mistakes, over and over. In fact, I can almost guarantee that, when I sit down to talk with a new client, I'll hear some version of the most common missteps.

A big part of what I do as a financial advisor is try to correct these investing mistakes, or avoid them altogether, and set clients on a more productive path.

What I hope to accomplish here, in some small way, is to give you that financial education you didn't get growing up. I'll try not to overexplain basic concepts; however, I want to be sure you understand the fundamentals. Because *it's the fundamentals that most people get wrong*. And that's what sets them on a lifelong detour away from wealth.

Many of us are walking around with huge gaps in our knowledge base. By the time we reach our thirties or forties, we're too embarrassed to admit that we don't understand how investing and financial planning work. That's what makes us so vulnerable to adopting flawed beliefs and habits. If you already know some of this material, think of it as a refresher course. If not, you'll be glad to learn it.

As you read this book, you're probably going to realize that you may not always make the best investment choices. That's all right. Don't feel foolish. Don't be ashamed. You are not alone. There's no shame in making mistakes. There is only shame in continuing to make the same mistake after you've learned a better way.

Wealth is not the huge mystery we make it out to be. It's not a hit-or-miss proposition. If you give yourself enough time and follow a few basic principles, you can and may have enough wealth to enjoy your unique version of happiness.

All that's really required is that you focus on a handful of strategies that can put you on the road to lasting wealth.

1

Don't Put All Your Eggs in One Basket

A few years ago I had a client, a mid-level executive, who held a high concentration of his portfolio in British Petroleum stock. When I sat down with him to hash out a financial plan, my main advice to him was that he should diversify. He had too much money invested in BP, and not enough in other assets.

But this client was not easy to persuade. He *loved* British Petroleum and, as a long-time employee of the company, felt fiercely loyal to it. And why shouldn't he? BP was a terrific, stable company. It was one of the world's half-dozen "supermajor" petroleum companies, with over a century of success and growth behind it.

I eventually got this client to agree that when the stock hit $80 a share, he would sell some of it. It wasn't the plan I recommended, but at least it was a plan.

One day BP's stock climbed to $79.20, so I called the client and said, "We're not at $80 yet, but we're pretty close. What do you say? Sell?"

"No," replied the client. "We need to be disciplined here." (Sometimes my clients like to throw my own words back in my face.) "It needs to hit $80 on the nose," he said. He didn't sell. Two days later, the Gulf oil spill happened. BP's stock plunged under $50 and, five years later, it still has not recovered.

I think you may see where I'm headed with this.

Let's look at a couple of other recent scenarios.

It's was the late '90s. Everyone, you may recall, was falling in love with high-tech stocks. All you had to do was put an "e-" in front of a company's name or a ".com" after it, and its stock would rocket up in price. Everyone thought everyone else was getting rich and was afraid to miss out on a historic opportunity. So individuals cheerfully abandoned basic investing tenets along with their faith in brick-and-mortar businesses. Value investing was left for dead. High-tech speculation was the new paradigm. The Internet became the new Wild West. Lots of people became disproportionately invested in tech stocks. And we all know what happened: The bubble burst. Many people lost everything.

A few years later, the pendulum swung the other way. Brick-and-mortar businesses came roaring back with a vengeance, in the form of residential real estate. People got bullish on buying houses, and started using their homes as bank accounts. Everyone was taking out leverage, borrowing against his or her home to buy *more* homes. Banks were throwing loans around like comedy club coupons in Times Square. Janitors now owned three condos. There seemed to be no limit to how high the price of housing could go. But the problem with real estate is that when a down market hits, you're stuck with debt service. You don't have the cash flow to manage those investments. Millions of people got a painful lesson about being over-invested in real estate and over-leveraged.

Concentration Is the Problem

The three scenarios above all illustrate one common theme: the dangers of having too much of your wealth tied up in one thing. This is known as concentration risk. Most people know about it, but it's still the biggest mistake I see clients make, hands down. It's an extremely easy mistake to make. Why? Because when a certain type of investment is doing really well, there's a strong temptation to throw as much of your money as possible at it to maximize your success. After all, if $1,000 in Facebook is good, then $100,000 in Facebook must be even better. Or so the thinking goes. And that strategy sometimes pays off beautifully . . . until it doesn't. The examples from history are many.

It comes down to this: The more your success, wealth, and/or happiness relies on one category of asset, the greater risk you are running. Why? Because if and when a change happens in the world, all of your assets will react the same way to it. They might react positively; then again, they might react negatively. The longer you carry a risk, the greater the odds of the latter happening.

The "too many eggs in one basket" error wears many faces. The three examples above illustrate some of the most common versions. The BP story is about being overly concentrated in your own company's stock. The tech-bubble example is about being overly concentrated in one particular market sector. And the housing example illustrates the dangers of focusing too much on one class of asset.

There are many other ways we over-concentrate—on one commodity, one country, one region, one person, one industry. If all your money is in airlines, for example, what happens if there's a prolonged pilots' strike, or if someone invents a new technology that *beams* passengers from place to place? If all your money is in Japan, what happens if Japan goes to war? If all your money is in beef, what happens if there's another mad-cow-type epidemic?

Change is the only constant. If a particular company, country, or sector of the economy is running hot right now, the one thing you can bet on is that someday it won't. But none of us—not the craftiest experts or the smartest researchers—can predict when that change is going to come. So keeping your wealth tied up heavily in any one thing, year after year, is a formula for loss. Eventually that one thing *will* experience a downturn, a disaster, or an unexpected challenge. And if you are over-concentrated in that asset, you will get hammered.

Of course, most of us don't *set out* to become over-concentrated in one asset. It typically happens gradually, often without planning. And it usually happens, again, as a function of success. The very success of an investment—whether it's oil, real estate, or a can't-fail company like Apple or Dell—is often what causes us to abandon sound investment practices. But we often don't even realize what we're doing until we wake up one morning with a portfolio that is seriously out of balance.

Diversification Is the Solution

The antidote to "too many eggs in one basket," as you probably know, is diversification. That is why the endless battle cry of the conscientious advisor is "diversify, diversify, diversify!"

To diversify means, essentially, to acquire a range of assets that will react differently to the same event. That is why a classic portfolio typically consists, at minimum, of stocks and bonds—because stocks and bonds generally react to economic trends in opposite ways. A negative event for stocks tends to be a positive event for bonds. All diversification is built around that simple principle. You try to acquire assets that are likely to thrive if your other assets suffer. In this way you protect yourself from severe loss. At least, theoretically.

When it comes to stocks, for example, if you're going to invest heavily in oil, then you should at least own stock in more than one oil company. That way, if one company runs into trouble, the other companies should pick up the slack and profit. But you should also consider what might happen if the whole oil industry runs into trouble, as it did in 2015. You might want to own stock in alternative energy companies, as well as in industries that can prosper when oil prices are low, such as airlines (when the price of jet fuel goes down, airline profits go up). But if, in turn, you own a lot of *airline* stock, you should also own stock in companies that can do well in the event of a downturn in air travel. Railroads, maybe, or virtual-meeting technology.

The idea is pretty simple and obvious.

But if diversification is such an obvious solution—and we all know it is—then why does the advisor's battle cry to diversify so often fall on deaf ears?

Because diversification, frankly, is boring. It's not fun or exciting. In fact, it can be a real wet blanket. Chasing the hottest new trend, on the other hand, can be positively thrilling. Watching assets make money hand over fist gets our blood pumping, and we naturally want to throw more and more of our money at the thing that is generating hot dollars. That's only human.

Diversification, conversely, is the voice of reason, caution, and adulthood. It's the voice crying, "Don't ski the expert trail; you'll break your neck!" We know that grown-up voice is right, but sometimes we don't want to listen to it.

Why Do We Load One Basket?

Why do otherwise rational people allow themselves to tie up more and more of their wealth in one type of investment, even when their rational minds know better? I'm not a psychologist, but in my experience there are several factors at play. It's wise to try to understand these influences a little, because, chances are, if you're over-concentrated, you're under the spell of one or more of them.

We get caught up in hysteria. Human beings are fickle creatures. We are *heavily* influenced by the behaviors and ideas of people around us. We don't want to be "the one who doesn't get it," and we often behave irrationally just to follow the crowd. Perhaps you've seen that experiment where a group of people (hired by the experimenter) gets on an elevator and deliberately faces the rear. A test subject placed in their midst often turns and faces the wrong way too.

Wall Street knows about this weakness in us and churns out marketing designed to make us feel that if we don't follow a certain financial trend, we are not in the know. When we see people around us gobbling up tech stocks or real estate, there is a part of us that fears we'll miss out if we don't jump on the bandwagon. We overrule logic and convince ourselves that becoming over-concentrated in the "hot" new asset is actually the rational thing to do.

We get swept up in the idea that we're riding the wave of the future, and that the old rules no longer apply. But the history of the market reveals that eventually everything reverts to the mean—what goes up, comes down; what gets hot, cools off; and what "can't fail," eventually does.

We don't want to admit we made a mistake. By the time we notice we've become over-concentrated in one thing, we may be in precariously deep. But we don't like to admit it. Behaving foolishly makes us feel ashamed. We don't like feeling that way, so we deny it by throwing good money after bad. I recall one client, for example, who put $100,000 into a certain investment vehicle for the purpose of avoiding taxes. But the whole deal looked rather sketchy to me. It appeared to be an obvious tax shelter, which I suspected the IRS would frown upon. So when I met with this person, I told him he was taking an unwise amount of risk. I believed the investment would likely pop up on the IRS's radar screen as a dreaded "listed transaction." I even brought in some experts to point out why he would likely get in trouble. Instead of taking steps to back out of his mistake, though, this person made a *second* large investment the following year. Sure enough, the transaction *did* get listed by the IRS, and he found himself seeking legal advice.

The more we have invested in a bad decision, it seems, the more reluctant we often are to admit a mistake. We double down on the bad behavior instead. The rational mind recognizes that we've made a mistake, but rather than cut our losses, we find a way to convince ourselves our choice was right—even when it's patently absurd.

Fixing a bad situation feels harder than living with it. In a similar way, we often live with an untenable situation because remedying it feels harder than acknowledging and correcting the problem. I recently spoke with a client who is in a family-run business. In this multimillion-dollar company, there is *no succession plan* in place for replacing the current, aging CEO. This is another type of concentration risk. The entire future of the company is riding on the health of a single individual. Everyone involved knows he or she needs an exit plan, but because of the family dynamics involved, it has become more palatable to take no action than to take the step of creating a plan of succession.

I can't tell you how many clients I've worked with who avoid the headache of diversifying by convincing themselves that everything's OK with their out-of-balance, over-concentrated portfolio. Denial is an extremely powerful psychological force.

We don't want to trigger a tax event. One of the main reasons we learn to live with a lopsided portfolio is that we dread triggering a tax event. We don't want to sell off any of our over-concentrated stocks because to do so would force us to pay taxes this year rather than down the road.

My advice is that it's better to just grit your teeth and take the tax hit now, especially if it's going to give you the benefit of diversification. You're going to have to pay the tax eventually anyway. Learn to see paying taxes as a badge of success, as many of my clients do. After all, you're only paying taxes because you *made money*. So pay the tax proudly and happily. Then buy some diversified assets.

13

You Can Diversify without Triggering a Tax Event

A great way to diversify without paying taxes is to do a CRT (Charitable Remainder Trust). Take a stock you're over-concentrated in, donate it to a charity, and get a nice tax deduction right now. Let's say the stock you donate is currently worth $1 million. The charity can sell that stock for its full value, paying no tax on it (because it's a charity), and proceed to pay you income on it for the rest of your life. And it pays that income on the full million, rather than on the roughly two-thirds of it you would have been left with (due to taxes) had you sold it yourself. When you and your spouse pass away, any principle that's left over remains with the charity. A CRT is a great win/win for both you and the charity.

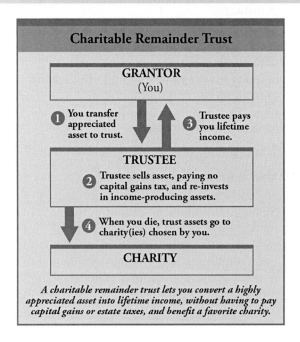

Charitable Remainder Trust

GRANTOR
(You)

1. You transfer appreciated asset to trust.

3. Trustee pays you lifetime income.

TRUSTEE

2. Trustee sells asset, paying no capital gains tax, and re-invests in income-producing assets.

4. When you die, trust assets go to charity(ies) chosen by you.

CHARITY

A charitable remainder trust lets you convert a highly appreciated asset into lifetime income, without having to pay capital gains or estate taxes, and benefit a favorite charity.

Success is self-reinforcing. When a behavior succeeds, it positively reinforces us. We want to do it again and again, like a mouse in a lab with a cheese dispenser. Investing is no different. When a stock is producing good returns, we want to continue buying and holding it.

I had a client, for example, who worked for a top high-tech company during that company's best six years. *No one* sold his or her company stock in that period. When I encouraged this client to sell some of his, he responded, "Why? The stock's doing great. Every quarter the company is beating its earning projections."

"That's *exactly* why you should sell some of it," was my warning. "That trend is not going to continue forever."

The company eventually had a major downturn and everyone who was heavily invested in it lost a fortune.

An asset's track record of success can make it seem downright crazy to not acquire more of that asset and hold onto it. Why drop a thing that is working?

Because of a well-known little principle called "buy low/ sell high." The way to make money on an asset is to buy it when its value is *under*-realized, not when it is running hot and selling for more than it's worth. When you're at the grocery store, do you stock up on coffee when it's at its highest price, or do you wait for it to go on sale? So why would you behave the opposite way with investments?

We want to max out our "winnings." One of the biggest reasons we don't sell an over-concentrated asset is that we fear we'll sell it before it hits its peak. We want to milk it for every last percentage point. But, of course, no one *knows* when a stock is going to peak.

Remember this: The pain of a big loss will outweigh any regret over not maxing out your investment for every possible percentage point. If you fail to get that last 5 percent, you'll be able to live with that. But if you lose *25 percent* by trying to wring out every penny? That's hard to live with. Especially if you have been warned.

The Warning Signs

So what are the signs that you may be over-concentrated in one asset?

First of all, your friends and advisors will tell you. I know that may sound simplistic, but because your colleagues and associates are not emotionally attached to the asset, they can often see the situation more clearly than you can. If people around you are telling you you're over-concentrated, do yourself a favor and listen.

Your gut will tell you, too. You will begin to get a gnawing sense of unease about the investment. Don't deny this or ignore it, and don't let the dread of paying taxes convince you to pretend you feel OK about it.

Here's a sure sign that it's time to diversify. Ready? It's called the Golf Course Test. If you find yourself on the golf course, bragging about the success of one of your investments, that's a sure sign that it's time to start moving on. As a famous book notes, pride goeth before the fall. We humans have a tendency to brag as a way of compensating for growing fears and doubts. So if you hear yourself boasting, consider it a red flag.

Of course, what it really comes down to is basic math. When you look at your portfolio and the percentages are out of line with what you've planned, it's time to make a change, no matter how in love you are with your concentrated assets.

Principles to Abide By

There are some simple steps you can take that will help you avoid concentration risk.

Have a plan and stick to it. The very best way to reduce risk and stay diversified is to have a well-thought-out plan for your assets and stick to it. As you may know, this is called an asset allocation. What it means is that you establish a certain number of buckets to put your investment money in, and you also set an optimal percentage of your money that you want to reside in each bucket. These buckets might be things like stocks (in general), employer stock, bonds/fixed income, real estate, and commodities. Everyone's portfolio should have *some* buckets. Minimal buckets, in my opinion, would be stocks, bonds, and real estate. As you acquire more wealth, you can add more asset classes and subclasses. A well-diversified portfolio may consist of many buckets to provide a broad range of market exposure. The percentage limits you choose to place on each bucket are unique to you and your circumstances.

But here's the key: *Stick* to the planned percentage limits for each bucket. Be ruthlessly disciplined about this. This involves a practice known as rebalancing. Every year—or at some regular interval—reset the amount in each bucket to the planned percentage of your total portfolio. This can be painful, because it entails selling the best performing assets and buying the poorest performers. Why? Well, when one type of asset is doing well, it grows relative to the other assets. It begins to occupy a larger percentage of your total portfolio than your plan called for. Stocks, for example, may have been 50 percent of your portfolio a year ago, but now they've done well and have grown to 70 percent. That means you need to sell some.

Rebalancing means that you sell some of the winners and buy some losers, returning your percentages to the planned limits. Selling winners and buying losers feels counterintuitive, but what it forces you to do is buy low and sell high, which is exactly what you want to do as a wise investor. Rebalancing not only helps you grow your money, but also helps you reduce risk.

Talk to an unbiased third party on a regular basis. At least once a year, perhaps more often, sit down with a knowledgeable person who has no emotional attachment to your finances. This might be a trusted financial advisor. This person can help you identify any overconcentrations in your holdings, and can also help you come up with a plan for correcting them. That might involve creating a charitable trust (see earlier sidebar) or selling the position slowly. Or perhaps your pension plan offers you an annual option of doing some diversification. Your advisor might encourage you to avail yourself of that option. A trusted advisor can also serve as a coach, reminding you to stick to the plan and to preserve the agreed-upon asset allocation.

We look to others for expertise in every area of our lives, from cooking a meal to buying a car. And yet, when it comes to our finances, we are often tempted to go it alone or read a few articles in *Forbes* and convince ourselves we're experts. A trustworthy pro can help us see and think more clearly.

Look at potential losses. One the greatest antidotes to overconcentration is to take a clear-eyed look at what the losses might actually cost you. Most clients, I find, are not risk-averse; they are *loss*-averse. When I sit down with a client who wants to invest in a particular stock, I typically show him or her the stock's potential drawdown—how far it could drop from its peak. When clients look at possible loss percentages in cold, hard cash, it can be highly sobering.

Keep an eye on trends. Though none of us can predict the future, we *can* keep an eye on obvious trends, and use that information intelligently. Many people, for example, have gotten heavily into bonds in recent years. Anytime interest rates go down, returns on bonds go up, so it hasn't been hard to make money in bonds over the last twenty years. But at some point it becomes a mathematical certainty that interest rates are going to hit bottom, and when they do, they have only one direction to go: up. If you have been overconcentrated in bonds, and you do not diversify when interest rates are nearing bottom, it is inevitable that you are going to lose money. The same is true if you are invested in a commodity that is growing scarce or in a technology that is obsolete. Don't let emotional attachment cause you to stick with an asset whose days are numbered.

There's a reason "putting all your eggs in one basket" is not a positive expression in the English language. If you put an entire collection of eggs into a single basket, what happens if you trip and fall, or the bottom drops out of the basket, or a strong wind blows the basket out of your hand? If you carry that basket around long enough, odds are, one of these events *will* occur.

2

Don't Try to Beat the Market

The "all my eggs in one basket" approach is based on a hidden—or perhaps *not* so hidden—belief: that a winning stock can *keep* winning; that it can beat the odds. There's another belief closely tied to this one. It's the idea that, over time, we can and should be able to beat the odds *with our whole portfolio*. In other words, beat the market. For many people, in fact, this is the very measure of successful investing. Did my portfolio or investment manager beat the market?

If you read the financial press, you will see one market-beating claim after another. Of course, firms can't come right out and say, "We can help you beat the market," because there are rules against that sort of thing. But they clearly *imply* it.

They trot out their market-beating results of the recent past and invite you to believe that you, too, can achieve such results if you sign with them. Though their ads may state, "Past performance is no indicator of future results," they urge you to believe the opposite.

But does anyone *really* beat the market, predictably and sustainably? And should beating the market even be a goal for the "casual" investor, not to mention the seasoned pro?

Active and Passive Investing

Let's look at two basic types of investing. These are *passive* and *active*. Passive investing is based on the belief that the markets are efficient. What that means, essentially, is that the markets generally reflect appropriate pricing for assets. Efficiency is ensured by the simple fact that every transaction has a buyer and a seller, and that both buyer and seller do their due diligence. If a car is worth only $15,000, no one's going to pay $30,000 for it. The market, in essence, reflects the sum total of all the buyer and seller intelligence that's out there. The passive investor's mind-set is, "Why spend your time trying to find inefficiencies in a system that is fundamentally efficient? Better to just invest in the market itself and let your money grow along with it."

Active investing takes a different approach. It is based on the idea that the market is *not* necessarily efficient, at least not completely so. The active investor's thinking is that if you do the right research and learn facts that others may not know, you *can* find mispriced stocks, and you can do so repeatedly. You can beat the market.

Alpha and *beta* are two terms you've probably heard. *Beta* refers to the returns of the market as a whole. So if the market produces 7 percent returns in a given year, and your portfolio also goes up by 7 percent, you can be said to have achieved beta. On a long-term basis, beta is just fine for the passive investor.

Alpha, in its simplest terms, refers to the amount by which you exceed the market's returns. So if the market produced 7 percent and your portfolio got 9 percent returns, you can be said to have achieved alpha of 2 percent.

The active investor chases alpha.

No One Beats the House

Many people believe they can produce alpha year after year, and many investment firms would like you to believe this. But, alas, no study has shown that people can achieve alpha over the long term. In fact, studies typically show the opposite. Morningstar, a well-known investment research outfit, has reported that fewer than one out of a hundred money managers actually beats the market for five years running. A 2014 article in the *New York Times*[1] suggests the figures are even stingier. A study was done in which 2,862 mutual funds were analyzed. The top 25 percent were identified and

1 http://www.nytimes.com/2014/07/20/your-money/who-routinely-trounces-the-stock-market-try-2-out-of-2862-funds.html

tracked. And how many of those funds remained in the top quarter for the next four consecutive years? Two. Out of 2,862. That works out to .07 percent; 99.93 percent of funds failed to consistently outperform the crowd.

Everything reverts to the mean.

A Callan chart brings this message home visually. Using color-coded squares, it shows how various investment indices have performed over a twenty-year period. I've heard it called a "quilt chart" because the squares, as you can see, form an almost random color pattern. Last year's winners tend to be this year's losers, and vice versa. What the Callan chart shows is that no type of investment consistently does well over a

The Callan Periodic Table of Investment Returns

Annual Returns for Key Indices Ranked in Order of Performance (1995-2014)

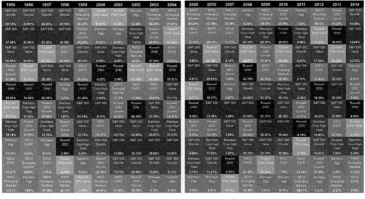

The Table highlights the uncertainty inherent in all capital markets. Callan's Periodic Table of Investment Returns depicts annual returns for 10 asset classes, ranked from best to worst performance for each calendar year.

Source: © 2015 Callan Associates Inc., Barclays Aggregate Bond Index, Barclays High Yield Bond Index, MSCI EAFE, MSCI Emerging Markets, Russell 2000, Russell 2000 Value, Russell 2000 Growth, S&P 500, S&P 500 Growth, S&P 500 Value

A larger size of this chart can be found on page 38.

prolonged period. So if you get into a vehicle that's working right now, and hope to beat the market with it for an extended period, the odds are not in your favor.

It is, in fact, extremely hard to beat the markets for even a *five-year* period (there's only one instance of this visible in the above chart). Over the course of many years, or a lifetime, it's practically impossible.

Which begs the question: Why pay for active management if virtually no one produces long-term results using this method? Why, indeed. Even if you argue that *some* money managers—a very small number, but *some*—are able to make alpha over a period of years, what are the odds that you will *find* that rare person in a sea of other managers who are all claiming to be able to do the same?

The Boring Truth

The boring truth is that passive investing—sometimes dismissed as couch-potato investing—is what actually works in the long run. Put your money in a well-diversified account, leave it alone, and let it appreciate. Period.

Studies (such as the famous Ibbotson and Kaplan study, *Does Asset Allocation Policy Explain 40, 90, or 100 Percent of Performance?*[2]) show that when you look at a large number of funds, over time, alpha sums out to zero. So where do

2 Ibbotson, Roger G. *"Perspectives: The Importance of Asset Allocation."* Financial Analysts Journal (2010): 1-3.

positive returns come from, then? Asset allocation. Put money in several different buckets and let the market work for you. Neither individual stock/bond selection nor market timing has any appreciable effect over time. Only the market itself delivers consistently.

If you take the Dow as an indicator, the market has failed to generate positive returns for only one ten-year period since we started tracking it. That was the so-called "lost decade" of 2000–2010. That period, as you may recall, encompassed both the Great Recession and the dot-com crash. It was brutal—the only ten-year period in which bonds beat stocks. If you left your money in the stock market for that decade, you basically broke even (and then you started making money again).

Though experts disagree a bit about long-term returns, most tend to agree that, figuring for inflation and other factors, stocks have earned around 7 percent, long-term, for the past 200 years. So beta's not a bad thing at all.

Anytime you try to beat beta, you take on more risk. If we say that the odds of getting market returns are 1:1, then to get better returns, by necessity, you must accept lower odds: 1:1.1, 1:1.3, 1:1.5, etc. Sometimes you might beat those odds for a while, but in the end, it's like Vegas. The house always wins, even if the odds are stacked only 50.5 to 49.5 percent in the house's favor. If you stand at the craps table long enough, you will go home broke.

By contrast, investing in the market is a little bit like betting with the house. Though the odds aren't fixed, as they are in Vegas, the chances are very high that if you cast your bet with five hundred highly rated companies—the S&P 500, for example—those companies, as a group, will grow and make money over time. So investing with the market greatly reduces risk.

But as you reduce your risk, you also reduce your ability to hit a home run, and that's where many people run into trouble. They want to hit that home run.

We Love Action and Hate Passivity

We are an action-oriented culture. Even the *word* "passive" carries slightly negative connotations. It suggests neglect or a lack of fighting spirit. We prefer to believe that by taking bold action, an individual can beat the odds, even if the evidence doesn't support that. Many active investors brag about their latest wins, but, like gamblers, they don't talk about their losses. If you look at the tax return of a typical active investor, and see how much money their investments made for them after taxes, you often find a story that's not so compelling.

Plateaus and slow periods are a natural part of investing. But we are uncomfortable with plateaus. Plateaus are boring. I confess to being a fitness fanatic, and when I hit a plateau in my workout results, I become restless. I want to make progress. Many of us are the same way with our money. When we see someone who is making money while we're flatlining, we want to jump ship and do what that person is doing. We become undisciplined. At the time of this writing, for example, the markets have been trading sideways for a while. Not surprisingly, BlackRock, one of the largest equity managers in the world, has reported movement of money out of its passive accounts and into its active accounts. People want to shake things up.

At the risk of sounding sexist, I must say this: Men are bigger shakers than women are, at least in my experience. Men love to tinker with things. Risk stimulates them. Their buddies give them tips or they read an article in the *Wall Street Journal*, and they want to *do* something. Women, by contrast, tend to make careful choices up front, then leave their money alone. Often when I look at a husband's and wife's IRAs, I'll see that after twenty years she has accrued substantially more capital than he has, and he was the one doing all the active management.

Investing is like weight control. Maintaining a healthy weight is about long-term discipline and sound lifestyle choices. But people get bored with this. They want to chase the latest quick-loss fad. So they spend money on coaches, weight-loss clubs, books, food plans, and exercise equipment. This gives them instant gratification, but usually only temporary results. Next year, the Pilates ball is in the yard sale, and they're on to something new. The real damage is that their weight seesaws up and down, which has a negative effect on their overall health.

Maybe we need to become more comfortable with the natural rhythms of life. Plateaus are normal, as are up-and-down cycles. Think about a marriage. Sometimes you are madly in love with each other, sometimes you are just good friends. If you ran out and had an affair every time your marriage became boring, you'd throw away everything you have invested in that relationship and you'd never realize its sweetest rewards.

Misunderstanding Gains and Losses

Much of the reason we fall in love with active investing is that we have misguided notions about gain and loss. We fail to appreciate just how difficult it is to consistently make positive gains. It's like standing at the craps table in Vegas and winning money hour after hour, day after day. It just doesn't happen. But we think we can beat the math, even when most of the great investing minds cannot.

The recent growth of the market has contributed to our misunderstanding. In the years between 2009 and 2015, many people have been seeing double-digit annual returns. As a result, they have come to regard this as normal. They may not realize that our economic recovery was engineered by skillful monetary policy. They now *expect* this kind of growth, and it's simply not sustainable. Investors need to understand that there will be 5 percent years, and worse, in the near future. Negative years perhaps. And they need to resist the temptation to abandon the patient approach during these times.

One reason we become impatient is that we mistake volatility for loss. Every time our stocks go down a bit, we think of it as a loss—one that should have been foreseen by our money manager—and we want to correct it. But volatility is not the same as loss. Volatility is a normal function of growth. Growth doesn't happen in a straight line. It's jagged.

Every day unpredictable things happen that no manager can foresee: natural disasters, nations defaulting on loans, scientific discoveries. These things affect the price of stocks, positively or negatively. But over time, solid companies do well and the market rebounds from dips. It always has.

Volatility is actually a good thing. Without these natural peaks and valleys, there would be no way to acquire assets at a low price and make money on them. When your stocks' value goes down because of volatility, remember, you haven't actually suffered a loss. Loss occurs only when you panic and *sell* your stocks at their lower price. If you just hold onto them—not blindly, but as a general rule—they will usually reset to their true value and your loss will eventually become a gain.

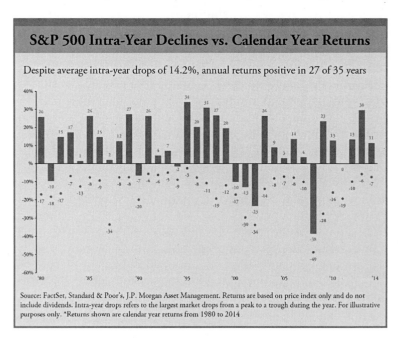

S&P 500 Intra-Year Declines vs. Calendar Year Returns

Despite average intra-year drops of 14.2%, annual returns positive in 27 of 35 years

Source: FactSet, Standard & Poor's, J.P. Morgan Asset Management. Returns are based on price index only and do not include dividends. Intra-year drops refers to the largest market drops from a peak to a trough during the year. For illustrative purposes only. *Returns shown are calendar year returns from 1980 to 2014

Timing the Market

Another misunderstanding that derails us is the belief that timing is at the heart of good investing. Marketers for the financial-services industry talk about timing and stock selection all the time. "Buy Apple now." "No, don't buy Apple; buy Google." "Make your move before it's too late!"

The financial media, which needs to sell newspapers and attract TV viewers every day, focuses on timing quite a lot. It gives their audience a reason to tune in on a daily, or even an hourly, basis. Stories about timing create wonderful suspense.

But in the long run, it's not very important which stock you buy and when. Google or Apple? Doesn't really matter. You just need exposure to technology in general. You should own Apple *and* Google, and several other tech stocks as well.

Market timers may score big once in a while, but not repeatedly and not over time. There are too many factors involved, too many things you can't know or control. What many people don't realize is that to make money by timing the market, you not only have to *buy* a stock at the right time—just before or after it hits bottom—but you also have to *sell* it at the right time, which means dumping a winner while it's still running hot. It's hard enough to guess both of these moments right with even one stock. But to do it over and over with multiple stocks and make money at it over a lifetime? Extremely difficult.

The house wins, except in fluke cases.

31

Technology Encourages Bad Habits

Timing the market has become a tremendous temptation because we now have the technology to get in and out of positions at the drop of a hat. Not so many years ago, if you wanted to invest in, say, a Brazilian mining company, you would have to fly down to Brazil with some of your business partners, check into a hotel, visit the site, talk to the management, then leave a partner on-site to make sure your money didn't disappear. And once you bought in, you might not be able to get out later. Today, a client can pull up an app on his iPhone while he's on the phone with me, buy some Brazilian gold Exchange Traded Funds (ETFs), then turn around and sell them by the end of our conversation. The liquidity is crazy, and it leads to some very bad habits.

Imagine if the real estate market were this liquid. Would you sell your house the instant you thought the market had peaked? Maybe you would if you had the tools and liquidity to do so, but that would be a very bad idea. Real estate almost always recovers within ten years.

Often the best action is to do nothing at all.

The Market-Beater Mind-set

Once you get it in your head that the goal is to beat the market, the tendency is to be discontented with slow growth and to make moves at all the wrong times.

A few years ago, a gentleman approached me to work with him. He worked for a high-end retailer where I was a customer. He had a modest nest egg and was having it managed by another firm. He wasn't happy with the firm's services. I tried to find out why, because history tends to repeat itself, but I couldn't get any clear answers. I finally agreed to work with him.

We came up with a financial blueprint customized to his needs and agreed to meet on a quarterly basis. It wasn't long before he started letting me know that he wasn't thrilled with the returns his portfolio had earned. He wanted more. I tried to educate him as to what sort of returns were realistic and possible, but it didn't sink in. Finally, on Christmas Eve, without warning and in fine holiday spirit, he sent me an email saying he'd decided to move his assets elsewhere.

What has happened to him since? Well, my firm's portfolio has outperformed that of the firm to which he moved. Soon he'll tire of that new manager and go somewhere else, but he'll never really get off the ground. I've seen this story a hundred times.

A portfolio, you see, is like an airplane. It needs to attain a certain ground speed in order to take off. Many would-be market beaters never get off the runway. They can't stick with one thing long enough. Before they even catch air, they see a new investment approach or management team that's having success, so they land the plane to chase after it. Every time they do this, they cause a taxable event, which further sets them back. And what they usually discover is that the hot new thing is now running out of gas and something else is catching fire. So they're forever moving at the wrong time and failing to gain momentum.

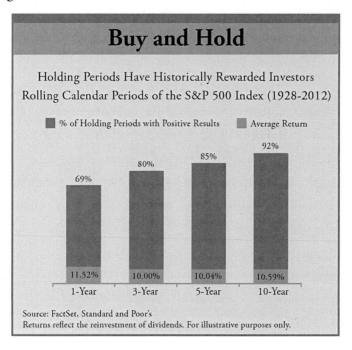

Buy and Hold

Holding Periods Have Historically Rewarded Investors
Rolling Calendar Periods of the S&P 500 Index (1928-2012)

■ % of Holding Periods with Positive Results ■ Average Return

69% — 1-Year — 11.52%
80% — 3-Year — 10.00%
85% — 5-Year — 10.04%
92% — 10-Year — 10.59%

Source: FactSet, Standard and Poor's
Returns reflect the reinvestment of dividends. For illustrative purposes only.

Learning to Work with an Advisor

Working with a skilled advisor can go a long way toward curbing such bad habits. But it's essential that both parties have clear expectations from the start. Many people, for example, are under the impression that it's the job of a financial advisor to beat the market. Not so. I often ask clients right up front what return percentage they are expecting. If they say 15 percent, I say good-bye and good luck.

For people who have been longtime active investors, it can be hard to learn to work with an advisor. Many active investors are diehard do-it-yourselfers. It's difficult for them to give up control and work with someone who employs a more passive approach. My ability to work successfully with such clients often comes down to whether they can accept what my true role is and perhaps learn to look at risk from a different perspective.

First of all, I tell clients that no advisor—no *ethical* advisor—can promise marketing-beating returns. This comes as a shock to some people; after all, if I'm not going to beat the market, what good am I? I try to explain that an advisor's role is to understand a client's life goals, to properly allocate assets so as to meet those goals, to assess risk, to figure out the liquidity needs of the client now and in future, and to put together a blueprint that addresses all of these needs. It's also the advisor's role to act as a support system. In times of stress or down markets, when the client wants to fold his tent and go home, the advisor can say, "We talked about this, remember? We knew that from time to time there'd be a market correction of 10 percent. Just hang tight. You don't need the money yet. So be patient. Stick to the plan."

In order to work well together, the client and advisor need to be in sync around goals and risks. They should ask and answer the question, "What are we striving for here: to die with the biggest possible pile of cash or to reach the goals in our blueprint?" If it's the latter, and we only need 6 percent returns to reach those goals, then we don't *need* to beat the market. Why are we going for 9 percent? Just to end up with more money?

It's crucial to understand that there is *much* more risk involved in going for 9 percent than in going for 6 percent. If you just want to reach your goals, why take more risk than necessary? Especially when trying to beat the market can actually cause you to miss some of those important goals.

Get-Rich Money and *Stay*-Rich Money

Some clients can't shake the active investor/market-beater mentality, and that's OK. What I tell them is that there are two types of money: *get*-rich money and *stay*-rich money. "Give me your *stay*-rich money," I say, "and you can hang onto the *get*-rich money." At that point we'll agree upon an amount that the client can safely play with. This is an amount that the client can afford to lose without negatively affecting his retirement, his kids' education, or his other major life goals.

I recommend you do the same. Leave your stay-rich money invested in the market, and try to *beat* the market with your get-rich money. It's like going to Las Vegas. Before you get on the plane, you set a limit on your fun money. Say, $1,000. You're OK with losing that much money (and if you win, it's all gravy), but you absolutely agree to stop betting once your thousand is gone. It takes discipline to do this, and some people don't have it. That's how they get into gambling—and investing—trouble.

The takeaway is this: Let the market be your bread and butter. Get it out of your head that you can or should beat the market on a regular basis. You can't. *But* if you find the idea of beating the market in the short term challenging, fun, and exciting, then by all means go for it. But only with your side money.

Full Size Chart from Page 24

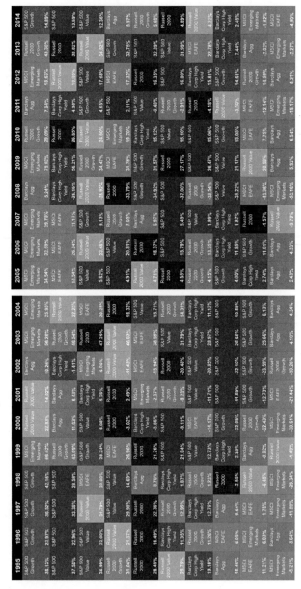

The Callan Periodic Table of Investment Returns

Annual Returns for Key Indices Ranked in Order of Performance (1995-2014)

The Table highlights the uncertainty inherent in all capital markets. Callan's Periodic Table of Investment Returns depicts annual returns for 10 asset classes, ranked from best to worst performance for each calendar year.

Source: © 2015 Callan Associates Inc., Barclays Aggregate Bond Index, Barclays High Yield Bond Index, MSCI EAFE, MSCI Emerging Markets, Russell 2000, Russell 2000 Value, Russell 2000 Growth, S&P 500, S&P 500 Growth, S&P 500 Value

3

Know Your Risk Threshold

Two questions I usually ask when I'm sitting down with a prospective client are:

- What was the best investment you ever made?
- What was your worst investment?

Typically, "worst investment" answers are more revealing than "best investment" ones, because the latter are often a matter of luck. "Worst investment" experiences usually come down to some version of the story, "I was sold investment x but I didn't expect y to happen. I was unprepared for what unfolded."

Recently, for example, a gentleman—let's call him Jake— was referred to my firm. I didn't even have to ask him both questions; his worst investment story was fresh in his mind. The moment we sat down, he began telling me how upset he was with his present financial advisor. Two or three years earlier, Jake had tasked this advisor with a tricky demand. Jake wanted to build a portfolio for income, but he had a limited amount of capital to generate his required income. So he needed a high level of income from this investment (this means we had to generate a high level of return for him . . . in order to get that high level of income).

A lot from a little, I thought to myself. *Sounds like a familiar tale.*

So the advisor put about two-thirds of Jake's money into Master Limited Partnerships (MLPs) that were heavily invested in oil and gas. I was not present at the meeting, so I do not know whether the advisor fully explained the risks of MLPs to Jake, but I will say that if I you need to generate high income on limited capital, then you need to include some risky vehicles. There's no avoiding it.

For the first year and a half, Jake's MLP investment did beautifully. It was churning out income like an ATM. With the increase of oil production in the U.S., the underlying value of the investment was going up, too. Life was good for Jake.

Until it wasn't.

In fall of 2014, oil prices dropped from over $100 a barrel to less than $50. Over 50 percent of wells in the U.S. were capped, and the value of oil MLPs went down the drain. Now Jake's investment was underwater, and he was crying foul.

Here I was, looking across my desk at yet another client who was in shock because he never thought the worst-case scenario would happen. I hate to say it, but I've seen it countless times.

"I Know There's No Return without Risk, But . . ."

Every investor knows the rule: *no risk, no return.* Many people, however, know it only as an abstract concept. They are often willing to take surprising risks in the name of getting potentially large returns. The reason, I believe, is that they often don't understand how real the potential for loss is. They haven't internalized it—quantified it in a way that they can feel and visualize. They focus almost entirely on the returns side of the equation, while denying or ignoring the downside.

This is partially the responsibility of an industry that promotes financial hope, but does not spend a lot of time preparing consumers for loss. It is also, to a large extent, the fault of investors themselves, who fall in love with high return rates without asking about the trade-off. Wherever the responsibility lies, the fact is that many investors today are walking around with a great deal more risk than they are consciously aware of. And they may only learn that harsh truth when their portfolio tanks.

It's critical to understand that loss *does happen.* That is why I work hard to quantify potential loss for clients. It's not that I want to put my clients in a negative mind-set, it's that I want them to truly understand that high returns have a price tag. Not everyone has the emotional makeup to pay that price. And that's OK.

Risk and Reward

There is no free lunch in the investing world. One principle that has always held water is that the higher the rate of return you are seeking, the greater the amount of risk you must be willing to accept. Similarly, when risk goes down—bonds, for example, are generally much less risky than stocks—so do return rates.

Again, physical fitness is an apt analogy. Everyone who sets foot in a gym knows the adage, *no pain, no gain*. But still, many people maintain unrealistic fitness goals. That's because they haven't taken a clear-eyed look at the price that fitness costs. Take, for example, the goal of having less than 10 percent body fat. Most people would probably love to push a button and award themselves a great muscle-to-fat ratio. But if you knew that the true price of attaining this goal would be to adopt a seriously modified diet, to limit yourself to no more than two alcoholic drinks per week, and to go to the gym six days a week, would you still be interested? There's no shame in saying, "No, that's not for me." There's only shame in fooling yourself into thinking you can have a super-lean body without paying the price.

Many of us do this with our financial goals. We all want to earn better than market rates on our investments. But how much volatility can we live with? How much drawdown? How much pain are we willing to endure to get this return? These are questions that are ignored by many advisors, and, consequently, by many investors. Until it's too late.

I believe in putting equal emphasis on both the drawdown and the potential gain. That way, the client—at least theoretically—is always aware of the investment's potential to drop in value. And so when volatility occurs, she is mentally and emotionally prepared. She doesn't panic and hit the "sell" button.

Standard Deviation and Drawdown

The industry has a few reasonably reliable methods for measuring the volatility of an investment. One of these is standard deviation (SD). Standard deviation tracks the extent to which an investment tends to deviate from its expected rate of return. More volatile investments tend to have a higher standard deviation, while more stable, "blue chip" investments tend to have a lower standard deviation. Standard deviation is used to predict, in essence, the reliability of future returns. Higher standard deviation equals lower reliability.

For every portfolio I offer a client, I do a standard-deviation analysis, which I present to the client in the form of a bell-curve chart. I won't provide the math that's used for SD here. If you are interested, it's very easy to find online, but let's look at how the SD concept can factor into a purchase decision.

The first thing most people want to know about an investment is its average return rate. This is an important number, but alone, it doesn't provide much information. You also want to know how the investment vehicle *behaves* in order to achieve that average. Each of the following sets of numbers, for example, produces an average of 5:

- 5 – 4.5 – 5.5 – 4.75 – 5.25
- 3 – 12 – 1.5 – 8 – .5

The first set produces its average without a lot of variance from the mean. The second set has a great deal more variance, or volatility.

A higher standard deviation denotes higher volatility, and therefore, a greater unlikelihood that an investment will achieve its expected returns for a given time period. So imagine you're trying to choose between two portfolios. Portfolio A has an 8 percent expected rate of return, and Portfolio B has a 10 percent expected rate of return. Both are considered "moderate" from a risk perspective. At quick glance, Portfolio B might seem like a better choice. But let's drill down a bit. Let's say Portfolio A has an SD of 15, while Portfolio B has an SD of 25. (I'm deliberately using high numbers for example purposes.) That means B is more volatile, less predictable, than A. We then calculate the drawdown, the largest amount each portfolio can be expected to fall. We determine that Portfolio A has the potential for a 10 percent drop every ten years, while Portfolio B has the potential for a 20 percent drop every ten years.

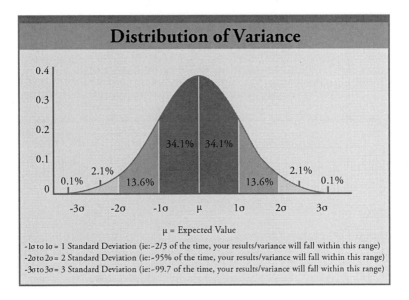

If your plan wouldn't survive a 20 percent drawdown, then why would you even consider Portfolio B? And if you get physically ill when your holdings suffer a 7 percent dip, how do you think you'll feel when they sink by 20 percent? Obviously, a 10 percent return is better than 8 percent, but can you and your plan endure the added uncertainty? That's the real question.

Are You Betting the Farm?

Unless you know the potential drawdown, you may be betting the farm on your investments and you don't even know it. I see many, many people doing this and it disappoints me because I know they are in for a potential shock. That's why whenever someone brags on the golf course about a great return he's getting, I ask him, "What's your potential loss?"

If he doesn't know the answer, that's a big red flag. It tells me he has been lucky so far, but may be due for a fall.

High returns go hand in hand with high risks.

Many people in Southern California (where I live), for example, got crushed on so-called second trust deeds during the housing bubble burst of 2008. When you buy a second trust deed, it means you're in second position on a piece of real estate. You get a higher rate of return—many people were happily enjoying 14 percent returns from these vehicles for a while—precisely because there's more risk: Namely, if something goes wrong, you'll get paid back only after the first-position party does. This arrangement works great when tenants are paying on time, and when the equity of the property stays positive. But when the value of real estate suddenly drops (eliminating the ability to refinance), when buyers start defaulting on loans, and when renters stop paying rent, positive cash flow can very quickly go negative. That's what happened to many people. The risks of second trust deeds were no doubt spelled out in the documents they signed, but when you're getting 14 percent returns, who can be bothered to read the small print?

The fact is that if you're achieving above-average returns, you are probably taking on above-average risk. The question is: Are you aware of that?

It's a Matter of Expectations

It's all about knowing how much risk you're taking and being comfortable with that. If you can watch an investment drop by 25 percent without flinching, then you'll be fine with a vehicle that has a 25 percent drawdown. But if you're carrying an investment with a 25 percent drawdown *and you don't know it*, you are likely to panic and do foolish things when that investment starts to do its downward dance.

That's essentially what happened in 2008. People were blindsided because they were taking on more risk than they were aware of, and the worst-case scenario happened. Many of these people missed out on the subsequent market recovery because they said, "Enough!" and got out of the market for good. On the other hand, when the Dow plummeted 508 points on "Black Monday," October 19, 1987, Warren Buffett's Berkshire Hathaway holdings dropped by a reported *$347 billion*. But Buffett did not jump out a window. Why? Because he was mentally prepared for such an event, so he held the course and didn't panic.

It is extremely important to understand two things at all times: (1) how much risk you are mentally and emotionally equipped to tolerate, and (2) how much money your present investments can potentially lose.

The way I define risk is the amount of volatility you are willing to accept over the long term. Think of it as your sleep quotient. Can you suffer a 20 percent drop in your portfolio and still sleep at night, or are you staring at the ceiling till 4 a.m. if you see a 3 percent drop? If you want a 10 percent return but you can't stomach the degree of volatility that goes along with that return rate, something needs to give. Either you need to increase your tolerance for volatility—easier said than done—or decrease your risk.

Investor Beware

When it comes to the loss potential of an investment, it's wise to adopt an attitude of *caveat emptor*. Sellers of investment vehicles love to talk about big returns, but not about downsides. So, ultimately, it's up to you to find out what you could possibly lose in an investment, to read the small print in the disclosure documents, and to take that information to heart. Losing your entire investment, or worse, might be a real possibility. How could you do worse than losing your whole investment? Well, you might get involved in a cash call. That's when the investees come back to the investors for more money, which can often happen in real estate development and venture capital deals. Suddenly, to protect your original investment, you have to put in even more money to prevent the project from going belly up. So you can find yourself throwing good money after bad.

You need to understand that the risks inherent in financial products may not be adequately explained or emphasized. That's why it's a good idea to work with an advisor, but only one with whom you have an open and trusting relationship. You and your advisor need to be clear on how much risk you can tolerate and how much potential loss is tied up in every decision you make together. As an advisor, I tend to bend over backwards to explain potential loss to my clients because I want to work with them for a long time and I don't want them to be surprised when a down market hits, as it inevitably will. Part of getting to know a client is to understand his or her sleep quotient. If there is too much risk in a portfolio for that particular client's constitution, then we may need to take some volatility off the table. In my view, it is perfectly acceptable to opt for lower returns in exchange for greater psychological comfort. In fact, to do so is often wise.

The Problem of Psychological Distance

It's important to keep the possibility of loss alive in our minds, so we don't unknowingly bet the farm on a given investment. This is tricky, though, because as human beings we tend to minimize risk. Every time we get into a car, for example, we risk death or injury. But we don't like to think about it, and that's healthy in some ways. If we focused excessively on the risk, we could become mentally paralyzed and never leave the house. On the other hand, if we allow ourselves to become psychologically numb to the dangers of driving, we can fall into bad habits, such as texting while we're driving. A certain amount of fear is healthy.

The closer we are to actual loss, the more real it becomes for us. You may have noticed, for example, if you go to the funeral of someone who dies unexpectedly, you find yourself thinking about things like life-insurance policies and wills. The same thing happens with investments. If you see a downturn in the market, you start to worry about protecting your investments. Conversely, the further away you are from negative market events, the less emotional weight you give them. I can tell you that the conversations I'm having with clients these days are very different from those I was having right after the financial crisis.

Risks also become minimized the longer we are exposed to them. We simply get used to them and they take up less room in our minds. People who live outside of Tornado Alley, for instance, can't understand how a person could comfortably live in Kansas, but most Kansas residents don't think about tornadoes too often. The same can be said for people who live along the San Andreas Fault, or in places where there are dangerous predators or disease-bearing insects. To outsiders, the risks seem huge; to insiders, the risks tend to fade.

This kind of psychological distancing can be dangerous in the world of finance. A major reason for the Stock Market Crash of 1929 and the Great Depression, for example, was the fact that banking and investing were comingled in unhealthy ways. Banks were taking too many gambles on the investing side, which put their overall stability at risk. So Congress passed the Glass-Steagall Act. Banking, investing, and insurance became separate entities. But then, about fifteen years ago, legislators decided Glass-Steagall was inhibiting competition. So the law was repealed. And we all know what came next. History essentially repeated itself. Banks took on too much risk in their investing arms, and 2008 happened.

The same thing happens with individuals. The further away you get from a negative incident, the less palpable it becomes, and the more acceptable the risk becomes. If a friend gets colon cancer, you might rush off to get a colonoscopy. But the longer you wait to act, the less likely it is that you'll do so. The risk fades from your mind. Similarly, the further away you get from a market event, the less you think about the risks inherent in your investments, and the more danger you court.

This is another reason for working with a good advisor. Left on our own, we tend to fall prey to psychological denial. It's human nature. But a good advisor can serve as a reality check. On a regular basis, an advisor can look at the risks in your portfolio, discuss them with you, and address them with effective countermeasures. The point is not that you should become nervous, but that you should remain fully aware of risk. Because, again, those who *expect* occasional stormy weather behave calmly and intelligently when it occurs.

Adopt a Goals-Based Model

There are a couple of steps you can take to help safeguard yourself against betting the farm on your investments. One is to practice goals-based planning, as opposed to the "He Who Dies with the Most Money Wins" approach. We talked about this a bit already. You and your advisor can work together to create a plan that helps you achieve your life goals with the least risk possible. If you're like most people, retirement income is the biggest piece of your financial plan. So figure out how much money you're going to need in retirement (we'll talk about this in more detail later) and then figure out what rate of return you'll need to get you there. Then aim for that. Don't take on any more risk than necessary.

Knowing what your goals are and how much downside (loss) you can tolerate tells you how much risk you can and should take on. Obviously, if you have more money than you need, you can accept lower returns and take on less risk than someone who has no margin for error and needs to get a higher return. The idea is that if you *need* to accept higher risk to reach your goals, then you do so, but if you don't, you don't. And if your plan calls for more risk than you can tolerate, then you must go back to the drawing board. Adjust your goals or find a way to add more money to the plan.

Be Wary of Short-Term Investments

Another practice you can follow is to be very careful about short-term investments. Short-term investments, by their nature, entail much more risk than long-term investments, yet many people don't seem to get this.

I often hear clients say things like, "I have some liquid money and I want to put it to work for a while."

I ask them, "When might you need that money?"

And the client might say, "Maybe in a year. I'm going to use it as a down payment on a house. Right now, the money's sitting in a bank earning nothing. I'd like to see it working harder."

I proceed to show the client the most conservative portfolio we have. I explain that the expected return is 5 percent, but the downside risk, over a one-year period, is 4 percent. "Is that acceptable to you?" I'll ask. "You have $100,000. Is it OK with you if it goes down to $96,000? Because that is a *very* real possibility."

In my experience, many people are willing to take far too much risk with their short-term money. It's as if they mentally take the inverse of the correct approach. "Hey, it's only short-term money," they tell themselves. "I wouldn't risk losing 4 percent with my long-term money, but with the short-term stuff, sure." In fact, though, it's the long-term money that can withstand the risk. For example, I have high confidence that the above portfolio will deliver its 5 percent returns over a ten-year period. But I have low confidence that it will do so over one year.

People want to be good stewards of their money, and th often feel that means they should *do* something with it. I once saw this sign in the window of a meditation s "Don't just do something; sit there." This advice is applicable to the world of investing. It is fine to le money alone and to be conservative with it, especi don't have a lot of tolerance for loss. In fact, I ev clients to just leave their money in the bank—y those minuscule interest rates. I know that fo the fear of losing their money makes their li that it isn't worth taking the chance.

Making money is a wonderful thing, but it just isn't worth taking an uncomfortable degree of risk to chase an extra percentage point or two. I would rather see clients play it safe than blithely gamble their life savings on risky investments without even being aware that that's what they're doing.

4

Making and Maintaining a Financial Plan

Recently I sat down with a client who'd had a liquidity event—selling a business—that had netted him an eight-figure sum. By most people's definition, he was set for life. He did live quite a "comfortable" lifestyle, but he could afford it. Or so he thought. But when we began to run his numbers, we soon discovered that his spending rate was so high, he would not be able to maintain it. If he didn't make some adjustments, he was going to be broke within a matter of years. "You have enough money to do anything you want," I told him, recalling a famous Buffett quote about leaving wealth to children, "but not enough to do nothing. You're going to have to make some choices."

This was a real eye-opener for the client.

Ultimately, we decided he would sell some real estate to raise some additional capital toward retirement planning, and also make some cutbacks in his lifestyle. It was hard pill for him to swallow.

Making a financial plan is sobering for people at all income levels. Many of us have a vague idea about where we want to go, financially speaking, but we are often reluctant to concretize a plan. That's because we know that once we quantify our goals and take a hard look at the way we're using our resources, we're going to have to make some tough choices. So we put it off.

Eventually, though, the weight of reality becomes too heavy to ignore. We realize we are going to have to get serious about money. With a mixture of trepidation and optimism, we gather our papers and seek out a financial planner.

Sitting Down and Getting Organized

One thing that still surprises me when I meet new clients is that their existing financial plan usually isn't a plan at all. Most clients, regardless of their net worth, have simply cobbled together a disjointed collection of financial . . . *stuff.* Some of the pieces may have worked pretty well for them, while others haven't.

These so-called plans are typically product-driven. At various points in the past, someone sold the client some financial products—insurance policies, investment products, limited partnerships, real estate, etc.—and they've all landed together in a heap without any sense of purpose or unifying philosophy.

What I also often see in these portfolios are one-off speculative investments. I call them high flyers. Maybe the client's brother-in-law talked him into a once-in-a-lifetime opportunity with a Brazilian diamond mine. Or the client decided to invest in a Hollywood movie or a real estate development scheme in Turks and Caicos. Two common components of these high-flyer items are hope and lack of liquidity. The client hopes the investment will pay off but has no way to get out of it.

After I review these financial grab bags, I ask the clients what they wish to accomplish financially. Often they look at me as if I'd just inquired about the price of peaches on Neptune. I see vague terror in their eyes.

It's my job to help them move from chaos to order. This can be mentally and emotionally overwhelming. People often want to freeze in their tracks or run out the door. And so I offer two pieces of reassuring advice:

Eat the elephant one bite at a time. It is going to take time to get a new plan up and working. Accept the fact that it's a process. Break it into small, digestible chunks, and feel good about doing the little things.

Keep it simple. Accomplishing financial goals doesn't need to be complicated. The simpler the plan, the more likely you'll stick to it.

Putting together a workable financial plan shouldn't feel like pulling teeth. Rather, it should provide a sense of calm, clarity, and peace of mind . . . once you get past the panic stage, of course.

The Planning Pyramid

The way I keep things simple is to use a planning pyramid. This is not a unique idea. If you've been around the personal-finances world, you've no doubt seen some version of the planning pyramid. Most versions consist of four or five levels, along with multiple subdivisions. The version I use is extremely basic and straightforward:

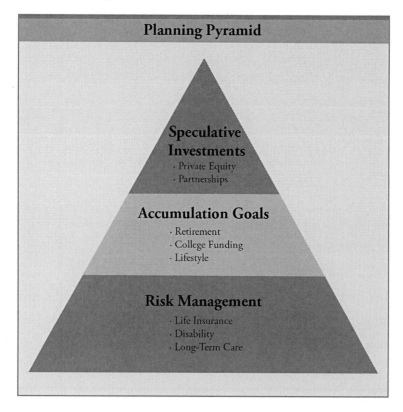

Planning Pyramid

Speculative Investments
· Private Equity
· Partnerships

Accumulation Goals
· Retirement
· College Funding
· Lifestyle

Risk Management
· Life Insurance
· Disability
· Long-Term Care

I keep the pyramid simple because I want my clients to imprint it in their minds and learn it by heart. As you can see, it consists of three levels:

1. **Risk Management.** The first level of financial planning is to protect yourself against the threats than can undo the rest of your plan.

2. **Accumulation Goals.** Level two is the "meat" of the plan, where you identify your important goals in life and figure out a strategy for achieving them.

3. **Speculative Investments.** After—and only after—you have taken care of the first two levels, you are now free to try to "beat the market," hunt for alpha, invest in your cousin's Hollywood movie, etc.

Because many people have had no education in financial planning, they flip the pyramid around and begin speculating before they've laid a foundation. Nothing could be less wise. Let's look at the three levels a little more closely.

The Foundation (Level 1): Risk Management

The foundation must come first. This is hard to accept because the base level is boring. It contains only the basic components. It's like the basement of a skyscraper; that's where they stick the parking facilities, boiler rooms, and maintenance equipment, not the fancy restaurants and luxury apartments. Risk-management devices are no fun at all, though they can be quite expensive. This is money we'd rather be spending elsewhere. But your plan's foundation is like a building's foundation in one other key way: Without it, the whole building would topple over in the first storm.

The point of laying a financial foundation is to make sure *your plan* does not topple over when challenged. There are three main setbacks your financial plan can face. These are: (1) that you die too soon, (2) that you get seriously sick or injured, and (3) that you live too long. Good basement-level planning means accounting for all three possibilities.

1. **Dying too soon.** The downside of dying too soon—other than the obvious one—is that you won't have accumulated enough assets to take care of your loved ones. Your death might leave your family in a financial deficit, with bills to pay and not enough resources to cover them.

The common way to address this is via life insurance. Make sure you have some. How much coverage you need and whether to buy term or whole life insurance are considerations you can discuss with a planner. We won't get into that here. But do buy substantial coverage and keep future inflation in mind.

2. **Becoming sick or injured.** An even worse scenario, financially speaking, is that you could become permanently disabled. In this case, you may be unable to work, but you might also incur ongoing expenses for your family.

To protect against this, you'll need regular health insurance, but you also might want to consider "extras," such as long-term care insurance and disability insurance. Long-term care insurance helps cover the added expenses that people who suffer from chronic illnesses and disabilities can incur—physical therapy, home health aides, and visiting nurses, for example. Disability insurance protects your income in the event you are incapacitated. This is essential if you are an entrepreneur or self-employed.

3. **Living too long.** The final threat to your plan's success is that you will live too long and run out of resources. This is a very real concern nowadays. Most people do not grasp the fact that retirement can now last for decades. The best solution to this is to create an inflation-proof retirement plan that can survive the down-market periods that will inevitably occur. We'll talk about this more in the next chapter. Guaranteed sources of income are also useful and important weapons for combating threat number three. These can include things like fixed annuities, pension plans, Social Security, and reverse mortgages. Many people try to use guaranteed sources of income to cover basic and routine living expenses.

There may be *temporary* threats to your plan, too. You might lose your job or face a huge medical expense. So when laying the foundation level, you should also think about how much liquidity you want. The lesson from 2008–2009 is that there is never enough liquidity. In addition to a healthy supply of emergency cash, you might want to think about lines of credit that can be accessed in a crisis.

The Heart of the Plan (Level 2): Accumulation Goals

Once you have laid a foundation, it's time to start thinking about the more interesting stuff: your short-, mid-, and long-term accumulation goals. What do you want out of life? Your goals are the heart of your plan; they're the whole reason for having a plan in the first place. They include things like a home, college education for your kids and/or grandkids, weddings for your children, a second home, a secure retirement, travel, inheritances, and philanthropic goals.

When dealing with the middle of the pyramid, the big shift most people need to make is to move away from a product-based plan and into a *goals-based* plan. Financial plans work only when they are based on goals we actually have. So the idea is to identify your main goals and then tailor a plan to achieve them (not to buy an assortment of financial products and hope they help you reach your goals).

To get a client's goals on the table, we implement a discovery process called *blueprinting*. This is something you, too, will want to do, whether you work with an advisor or not. The idea is to sit down—with your spouse if you're married—and download all of your goals onto paper. What you may find surprising is that you and your spouse may have differing goals and priorities but you never knew it because you never sat down and spelled them out.

The next thing you do is look at all of the resources you have accumulated thus far, as well as those you are likely to accumulate.

In most cases, it quickly becomes obvious that the goals exceed the resources, so you need to prioritize. What I do with clients is divide goals into *must-haves* and *nice-to-haves*. A wedding for your daughter might be a must-have. Your desire to host it at the Ritz Carlton, though, might be a nice-to-have. Wedding bells may need to ring at the Elks Lodge in order for you to achieve your other goals.

The next part of planning can be complicated in practice, but it's simple in principle. Once you've captured your goals and put them into priority categories, apply your financial assets against them. As part of this process, you will look at the return rate you need to earn on your investments in order to accomplish at least your must-haves. You might determine, for example, that you need a 6 percent average annual return, after fees and taxes, to make your big goals happen.

Finally, you look at return expectations. Why? Because you need to have reasonable faith that you'll be able to achieve that 6 percent return rate over the long run and that your plan will survive stormy waters along the way.

At my firm we stress-test every plan.

Stress-Testing Your Plan

Traditionally, advisors use straight-line return assumptions when making financial plans. This assumes a steady annual rate of return year after year. But of course, we all know that nothing moves in a straight line. It is the *way* your returns occur in reality that can determine whether a plan is viable or not. That's why we use three sets of calculations.

1. **Straight-line analysis.** We start with the straight-line method because this can be helpful in determining certain outcomes and projections.

2. **Worst case.** We next assume two back-to-back negative market years as soon as you retire. We ask the following question: *If your plan lost 35 percent of its capital, could you survive?* In 2008, many people couldn't. They had to make drastic lifestyle adjustments as they headed into retirement.

3. **Monte Carlo simulation.** Finally, we employ software to create a variable return scenario. The program we use crunches through 10,000 possible iterations of your returns, based on historical data, and offers a range of outcomes. The worst outcome, of course, is that your plan fails; the best is that you meet all of your goals and have a ridiculous amount of money left over when you die. Results in the middle are the most likely. Using the range of results the program spits out, we calculate a "confidence meter" for your plan. My litmus test is that I like to see a minimum of 85 percent of the 10,000 trials coming out successful. If you have the available assets, we can go for an even higher confidence level (we can never get to 100 percent, though).

So a good plan is goals-based and also accounts dynamically for the probability of success. A good financial advisor can add a lot of value here; most average people don't have the capability of calculating all these probabilities and adjusting for them.

Putting Speculation in Its Place (Level 3)

Now we get to the top level of the pyramid. Here is where we start to think about speculation and decide what place it can have in the overall plan.

Speculation—investing in risky highflyers—is not a bad thing. In fact, for many people, this is where investing becomes fun and interesting. The key is to do your speculating in the context of a sound, risk-managed plan with a high confidence-meter reading. If you're comfortable from a risk perspective, and all of the goals in your plan are being properly funded, then, by all means, feel free to roll the dice on your neighbor's new microbrewery. How much money should you put into highflyers? Well, it depends on your taste for risk. But the test is simple: If you lose *all* of the money you're risking, it won't upset the pyramid.

It never ceases to amaze me how many intelligent people flip the pyramid upside down. The first chunk of money they get their hands on goes into the speculative piece. Professional athletes famously make this mistake. The moment they receive their signing bonus, they invest in a nightclub or an orange grove in Florida. And inevitably, they're broke at the end of their short careers.

Spending Too Much

Another mistake pro athletes and entertainment-industry individuals make is buying a Malibu mansion and a collection of imported cars. Many doctors, lawyers, and businesspeople fall into a similar trap. They ratchet up their lifestyle as soon as their income increases. They move to a bigger house, buy a nicer car, and join the country club. They spend at the maximum end of what their income can support.

But this is the opposite of how to build wealth and achieve financial goals. It is actually people who plow most of their money into their financial plan who become wealthier and happier in the long run. They may not be flashy, but they achieve the goals that matter to *them*, while also putting themselves in a position to help their children, their parents, and their favorite philanthropies. And when a market downturn occurs, they have the resources to weather the storm without having to sell the clothes off their backs.

Social psychologist Leon Festinger said that social comparison theory suggests that humans derive their sense of self-worth by comparing themselves to others. When we are surrounded by people who own swimming pools, for example, we want to be part of the club, so we go in hock to buy one too. In the community where I live in Southern California, an unspoken game of *Who Can Own the Priciest Car?* is in play.

But if you want to develop true wealth, you would be wise to make an inner shift. Learn to derive your satisfaction from funding your plan, not from outspending your peers. In their eye-opening book *The Millionaire Next Door*, authors Thomas J. Stanley and William D. Danko assert that the truly wealthy do not live in Beverly Hills and drive Bentleys. Rather, these "closet millionaires" live below their means and hew to the belief that financial independence is a much worthier goal than social status.

Having a financial plan that you believe in—one that excites and energizes you—is the best way I know of to shift from a *spending* mind-set to an *accumulating* mind-set.

A Plan Tells You How to Behave

One great thing about having a plan is that it tells you what to do with your money. You don't have to agonize about it. If you have a good year, for example, you don't need to run around looking for a place to put your extra income. You just look at your plan. Your core investments and satellite investments are preselected, so if you earn an extra $100,000, you can just put $60,000 here, $20,000 here, and $20,000 there. No stress. High confidence.

A plan also allows you to stop and ask, "What impact might this extra money have on my goals, risks, and probabilities?" The cash can do several things for you, depending on your preferences. You might decide you can now lower your plan's risk factor, because with the extra money, you don't need as high a return rate as you did before. Or you might decide you can retire earlier or live a better lifestyle during retirement. The point is that a plan allows for personal preferences, but gives you a tool for weighing and analyzing decisions.

Again, the fitness analogy comes to mind. If your goal to is to reach a certain target weight by a certain date, and you beat your weight-loss objective for the week, you now have some choices you can make. You can "bank" the extra weight loss in case you have a bad week in the future. You can try to reach your target weight sooner than planned. Or you can decide that you're going to eat a piece of that chocolate mousse cake you've been craving. You can afford it now.

The same thing happens with a financial plan. When you come into some unplanned money, you might decide that you want to buy a Mercedes. Or you might decide that putting the money into your plan gives you more joy than buying a car. There's no right or wrong choice, but it's the plan that provides the context for making an intelligent decision.

Your plan also gives you a context for dealing with setbacks and bad years. When things don't go well, it lets you ask, "What course corrections can I make to get back on plan?" and provides you with a ready set of options.

Sustainability Is the Key

Sticking to a financial plan is far from easy, especially at first. So you'll want to do everything in your power to make the plan *sustainable* in your life. There are a few actions and attitudes that can help with this:

Understand that planning is worth the time and effort.
Yes, planning will be painful and overwhelming at the start.
But one thing I can absolutely assure you of is that goal-driven
plans *do* produce long-term results. Product-driven plans
don't, at least not consistently and predictably. Have faith in
the plan. Believe.

Get some support. Consider working with an advisor.
A good advisor not only provides expertise and experience
you don't have, but also gives you an accountability partner.
A year from now, this partner will remind you of the goals
you said were important to you and will make sure you are
honoring the plan.

Look forward to the results. When in doubt or feeling
undisciplined, focus on your goals—such as owning a second
home, having an adventurous retirement, or seeing your
daughter receive her law degree—and *feel* them emotionally.
The more you internalize your goals, the more likely you are
to stay disciplined.

Get in sync with your spouse. It is said that the number-
one cause of conflict in marriages is money.[3] As a result, many
couples never talk about it. But avoiding the topic doesn't
relieve the conflict; it just redirects it. It is much better to
get money goals and priorities out in the open. You and
your spouse can do this on your own, but going to a trusted

3 "New Survey Reveals: Money Number-One Cause of Conflict for Engaged
Couples, Newlyweds and New Parents." *PRNewsWire*. August 22, 2012.
Accessed November 4, 2015.

advisor may be better. Financial counseling is like marriage counseling. It gives you a safe place to talk about money. It also allows you to make compromises and iron out your differences, so that whatever plan you make has the 100 percent backing of both of you.

Austerity is not the goal here. Having watched countless plans succeed and others fail, I offer this word of warning: Don't be so "all in" with your plan that you make your life miserable. Allocate some money for fun. We've all seen people who starve themselves or curtail their credit card spending for six months, and then binge to make up for the deprivation. If your plan has no room for enjoyment, there's a high chance you will sabotage it at some point. It is much harder to come back to discipline once you have lost it. So try to keep a balance. Moderation will sustain your plan better than turning it into an extreme sport.

Studies—for instance, one done by Dr. Gail Matthews at Dominican University of California[4]—strongly suggest that people who write down their goals and track those goals have a much higher likelihood of achieving success. Making a written financial plan has some great side benefits too. It can help you root out inefficiencies in your spending and reduce fees and waste. It may also inspire you to deal with other important life matters you've been putting off, such as writing a will and setting up a trust.

---

4 http://www.forbes.com/sites/ellevate/2014/04/08/why-you-should-be-writing-down-your-goals

One thing is for sure: If you succeed without a plan, it will be in spite of your financial behavior, not because of it. Is that a gamble you want to take with your family's future?

5

Assess Your Longevity Risk

Greece is a magnificent country. I've spent time there, and it's a hard place to leave—the jewel-blue ocean water; the sense of history; the fresh, delicious Mediterranean food; and, of course, the people. There's a passion and a *joie de vivre* about the Greek people that is utterly infectious. As I write this chapter, though, the beautiful nation of Greece has gone bankrupt and is wrangling over its third bailout agreement. What went wrong?

Well, one of the main reasons Greece *is* such a vibrant, healthy, and life-affirming place is that its social system places a high premium on quality of life. For years, Greece has allowed its people to retire as early as 50; the majority of Greeks retire before 60. But therein lies the problem. With all that clean air, good wine, and fresh food, Greece's people are simply living too long for the pension system to keep up. It has collapsed under the weight of its obligations.

This problem is not Greece's alone. We are experiencing it on the other side of the Atlantic as well. When you look at American unions—such as teachers' unions, for example—you see their pension plans facing similar struggles. They are running at a deficit. These plans were designed thirty, forty, fifty years ago, when people just didn't live as long. Their funding cannot keep up with their payouts. Social Security, as we all know, faces similar challenges.

The problem is a simple but vexing one. People are living longer, healthier lives. And while this is great news for humanity in general, it is bad news for retirement plans. No one put this in the budget.

Longevity is becoming a huge financial dilemma. Who is going to pay for it, and how? How do we support ourselves when our period of *living off our resources* lasts almost as long as—or longer than—our period of *generating resources*?

It's not just a social question; it's also an individual one.

Businesses Have Shifted the Burden onto Us

Ever since World War II, businesses in America and many other countries have been smartening up to this issue, by necessity. As life expectancy climbed steadily upward in the 20th century, pension plans were being put under greater and greater strain. The writing was on the wall: The system was unsustainable. Corporate America began to look at pension plans as liabilities.

And so a major shift began to occur, from *defined benefits* plans to *defined contribution* plans. Under the old defined benefits plans, retirees were guaranteed income and medical benefits for life. Under the new defined contribution plans—such as 401(k)s and profit-sharing plans—it has become the responsibility of the employee, not the employer, to ensure that her retirement plan is adequately funded. Corporations have wriggled off the hook.

As the following chart shows, the shift has been dramatic. The graph charts the movement, from 1979 to 2011, away from defined benefit plans (•♦•) and toward defined contribution plans (—■—).[5]

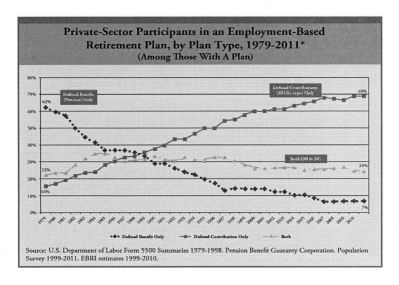

Source: U.S. Department of Labor Form 5500 Summaries 1979-1998. Pension Benefit Guaranty Corporation. Population Survey 1999-2011. EBRI estimates 1999-2010.

---

5 http://www.ebri.org/publications/benfaq/index.cfm?fa=retfaq14

Within a few short decades, the responsibility for taking care of our retirement has shifted away from companies and unions and onto us as individuals.

Unfortunately, many people have not internalized this shift. Intellectually, they know they need to assume ownership for their own retirement planning, and yet they haven't gotten serious about making the numbers work. In particular, they have not gotten serious about longevity. As human beings, we simply are not wrapping our heads around what it means, financially, to live as long as we are now living. The risk is no longer that we'll die too soon, but that we'll live too long.

The Thirty-Year Retirement

Maybe you've seen one of those Prudential billboards announcing, "The first person to live to 150 is alive today." It's an attention-grabber, for sure. Another sign I've recently seen proclaims, "One in three children born today will live to 100." Similar statistics are everywhere. Here's one we often hear in my business: "For every couple in their mid sixties today, one of them will live past age 90."[6] Life expectancy has been increasing by two and a half years every decade. To put it another way, for every hour we're alive, our life expectancy is increasing by fifteen minutes![7]

6 http://articles.baltimoresun.com/2011-06-05/business/bs-bz-ambrose-assumptions-20110605_1_retirement-planning-assumptions-investment-firms
7 http://www.economist.com/news/finance-and-economics/21613335-new-financial-instruments-may-help-make-pension-schemes-safer-my-money-or-your

One of the greatest challenges I face as a financial advisor is to get my clients to understand the reality of longevity risk. Most of us are so busy handling the problems of today that we barely have time to think about retirement at all. And when we do think about it, we use the only models we know: our parents and grandparents. We think of retirement as golf and travel and lazy games of bridge. Our grandparents, though, only lived five or ten years in retirement. Our parents retired at 65 and lived to maybe 83. Both of those generations had pension plans, reliable Social Security checks, and money in a savings account that earned enough interest to keep ahead of inflation. It's not terribly hard to live the golfing life when you have steady resources and your retirement is relatively short.

Today, most of us don't have pensions, Social Security is under constant assault, and savings accounts pay negligible interest rates. And we're not living eight or even eighteen years in retirement. We're living thirty years, or more. It's a completely new reality we're facing. The old model has gone out the window.

I'm not trying to alarm you. What I am suggesting is that—busy as you are and unpleasant as the topic may be— you must put some serious thought into how you are going to support the long life you are now likely to live.

Understanding Life Expectancy

When I sit down with a client to do a financial blueprint, we look at the three big financial threats I talked about in the last chapter. By far the most daunting of these is the third one: that I will outlive my money.

It's crucial to get this one right. That's why my firm tries get as accurate a prediction for clients as possible. One of the tools we use is a computer program. It asks a series of questions, such as: "Do you exercise regularly? Did you ever smoke and do you smoke now? How old were your parents when they died?" And it calculates your life expectancy. In your case, for example, it might be 87.

It's tempting to latch onto this number and use it for your planning. But what you need to understand when looking at life-expectancy numbers is that 87 is only a mathematical mean. There's a 50 percent chance you'll die before this age, but there's also a 50 percent chance you will live longer. And as you get closer to that age in reality, your life expectancy moves outward. You become statistically more likely to be one of the long-term survivors. What this means is that, when doing your planning, you need to account for living longer than your expected age.

This is something many people get wrong in their planning. You need to plan as if *you're going to be in the 50 percent that lives past the estimate.*

What Are the Risks?

The risks of outliving your resources are quite real, even given *today's* life expectancies. But life expectancy is a moving target. None of us knows what medical breakthroughs lay around the next corner. If you're 35 now, it is hard to say how

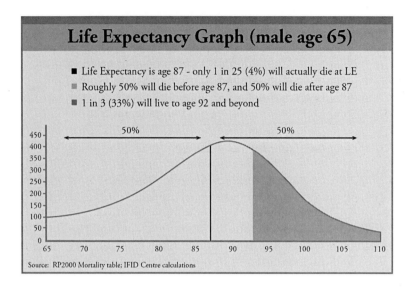

Life Expectancy Graph (male age 65)

- Life Expectancy is age 87 - only 1 in 25 (4%) will actually die at LE
- Roughly 50% will die before age 87, and 50% will die after age 87
- 1 in 3 (33%) will live to age 92 and beyond

Source: RP2000 Mortality table; IFID Centre calculations

long you might actually live. It seems unlikely, though, that life expectancy will go down—barring some great natural disaster or epidemic. The trend is moving ever in the opposite direction. Up, up, up.

The risk to you is that you won't be able to meet your expenses. When thinking about late-life expenses, you not only have to think about everyday needs, such as housing, food, medical care, transportation, and recreation, but you also have to take long-term care into consideration. Long-term care is the new X factor. This was not a huge factor in previous generations, mainly because the elder years did not last as long. People got by with a combination of in-home care provided by family members and perhaps a few years in a nursing home. But now, with most of us living longer lives, more graded and long-term options are needed.

If your town is anything like the area I live in, you probably have noticed a new breed of facility popping up like mushrooms after a rainstorm. These are senior-care communities, many of which have a combination of assisted-living and nursing-care facilities on the same campus.

The new model for elder living is a four-step process: (1) You live in your own home, unassisted, for as long as possible. (2) When you are no longer capable of living without assistance, professional in-home services—such as a visiting nurse or home-care aide—are arranged. (3) The next step is assisted living, in which you live in your own apartment on a campus, and services and monitoring are available around the clock. (4) When you need more constant supervision or medical care, you are transferred to the nursing-care facility, which is usually the last stop.

All of this can be quite expensive. Facilities can run about $8,000 a month. The risk to you, as a retiree, is that you will have to pay for it. This creates enormous exposure for your financial plan. You can burn through your assets very quickly. Diseases such as Alzheimer's represent a worst-case scenario, because you can remain physically healthy for many years, while still requiring a high level of care.

Managing Longevity Risk

Longevity risk *can* be managed, but the earlier you start planning and the more resources you can commit to it, the better. There are a couple of basic approaches to doing this: You can assume the risk yourself or you can transfer the risk to another party.

Assuming Longevity Risk

If you assume the risk yourself, the first thing you need to decide is how long you're planning to live. That might sound odd, but you do need to pick a number, based on an educated guess. It should be a conservatively high guess, keeping in mind that half of all people beat the average. The age you select tells you how long your plan needs to last.

You also need to make some essential philosophical decisions. Is your ideal goal to be spending your last nickel at the moment you take your last breath? (Maybe you've seen that bumper sticker on a pricey car, "I'm spending my kids' inheritance.") Or do you plan to leave a financial legacy behind? Each of these scenarios suggests a different level of aggressiveness in your planning.

Now your job is to ensure that you have sufficient assets, and that you will be able to grow them at a sufficient rate of return, so that you will have enough cash flow through the entire plan period. The earlier you start on this, the better, thanks to the incredible power of compounding (we'll talk about this in a later chapter). Many of us wait until we're in our fifties to get real about retirement planning, but if we were to start in our twenties, it would be so much easier and less painful.

Transferring Longevity Risk

The other approach is to transfer longevity risk to another party, such as an insurance company. One way to do this is through long-term-care insurance. This product can help cover the costs of in-home care, adult day care, and assisted-living and nursing-home care. As you may know, though, long-term-care insurance has run into problems recently. Insurers have lost money on it, so premiums have gone up, benefits have been reduced, and fewer companies are carrying the coverage. But it is still a viable way to help protect your assets from being eaten up by care costs, if you can afford it.

Another option is to purchase one of the various annuity products available. In this case, you give up some of your assets in exchange for a lifetime of income. You pay the provider (often an insurance company) a fixed sum of money, and the provider pays you income for the rest of your life. This is a gamble of sorts, for both parties (but, of course, the odds favor the provider, much as the odds favor the house at a casino). If you live a long time, then you "win" because you collect a large number of payments; the insurance company "loses." If you live only a short time, then the insurance company wins because you collect only a small number of payments. Annuities can be paid for over time or in a lump sum. Either way, substantial assets must be committed to fund a substantial annuity.

I often use a mixture of *assumed* longevity risk and *transferred* longevity risk for my clients. I like to use transferred risk—i.e., annuities—to cover fixed costs, such as housing, food, and utilities. That way, my clients will always be able to pay for their necessities, no matter how long they live. Then I like to use assumed risk—i.e., portfolio returns—to pay for variable costs. Variable costs are the fun things like vacations and theater tickets. So when you have a good year of returns, you get to do more fun things, and when you have a bad year, you cut back on the fun stuff. It's kind of like getting a bonus during your working years.

This combination of approaches protects your necessities while allowing you to enjoy extras as you can afford them.

Inflation—the Other X-Factor

Human longevity has thrown another monkey wrench into financial planning: inflation. Inflation is a more critical consideration than it was in the past. Many of us don't give it its due weight, however. When doing our financial planning, we often fail to adequately account for two huge inflationary periods. One of these occurs between the present day and the day we retire; another occurs between the day we retire and the day we die. Expenses that cost us $25,000 at age forty might cost us $65,000 by the time we retire, and $150,000 by the time we die, another thirty years later. Longevity and inflation.

Traditional planning says that as you get older, you ratchet down your financial risk until all you own are municipal bonds. But that strategy doesn't work anymore. Leaving money in safe, low-return vehicles won't stay ahead of inflation. With potential thirty-five-year periods to plan for, you *must* take some risk. (I'm talking about simple financial risk here, not longevity risk.) In today's retirement landscape, taking too little financial risk is as big a mistake as taking too much.

How much risk do you need to take? It depends on your exact circumstances, but basically, you need to keep up with inflation plus a few percent more. If we agree that inflation is 4 percent, then you might need to get 6 percent, plus another percent to cover fees and expenses. So that's 7 percent. Which means you will need to take some risks. You can lower this risk a bit as you get older, but not by as much as you used to.

An Offset to Risk

The good news is that with the help of a skilled planner, you can offset that risk somewhat. How? By using a three-bucket system.

What you do is put your next one to three years of income needs in your liquidity or ultra-low-risk bucket. Try to have cash or other highly liquid instruments on hand to cover this period. This bucket doesn't really care what the market does. Next, you have a middle bucket for your three-to-five- or three-to-seven-year needs. Here is where you can take some moderate risk. Finally, you have a seven-year-and-beyond bucket, where your highest-risk vehicles reside.

The idea is that if there is a market downturn, your long-range bucket has time to recover. You're not planning to sell from it for at least seven years. Historically, the market takes two to three years to bounce back, so there should be plenty of time for it to rebound. By using buckets, you are simultaneously able to take the risk you need in order to beat inflation, but also insulate yourself from that risk so you can sleep at night, and you're not tempted to sell at the worst time possible. You can plan better and sell assets in a much more advantageous way.

A good planner can help you strategically manage your buckets.

An Offset to Inflation

Today, many financial planners talk about inflation as if it's a runaway train. Looking at longevity, then adding compounding for inflation, they talk about our financial expenses as if they will constantly increase until the day we die.

But while we do need to take inflation very seriously, there is one factor that offsets this: Our spending tends to decrease over the course of retirement. Many financial advisors have observed that the thirty-year retirement period tends to fall into three distinct periods.

The first period is made up of what are called the "go-go years." This is when our enthusiasm and energy level are highest. We are excited by retirement and by doing all those things we couldn't do during our working years. We travel, we take painting lessons, we go to restaurants and concerts with friends. The go-go years are when we spend the most money.

Next come the "slow-go years." The novelty of retirement starts to wear off. Health issues start to creep in and we begin to slow down. Suddenly, getting on a plane seems like more work than it did before. Watching a movie at home seems more appealing than going out to the theater. Our spending goes down.

Finally come the "no-go years." Physically, we don't do much anymore. We may be dealing with some major health setbacks. Our variable costs shrink even further, and we don't travel anymore. Psychologically, we move into an internal place, where memories and spiritual fulfillment hold more meaning than expensive outings. My mother, for example, at age eighty-one, has reduced her spending to the point where she has been accumulating a surplus for the last few years.

One caution to keep in mind is that our largest medical expenses often come during the last few months and weeks of our lives, as doctors scramble to keep us alive a short while longer.

The New Retirement

If you think of retirement as thirty-five years of golf and travel, the financial implications are staggering. How do you support such a juggernaut? But the truth is that most people don't even want that kind of retirement anymore.

I've observed, among my peers, that people are not just living longer, but also working longer. It could be argued that this is because they need to financially, but there's more to the story. Many are working longer because they want to. They still have energy and enthusiasm and would rather "wear out than rust out."

I have a friend, for example, who received a windfall and retired early. At first he did some work on his houses, took exotic trips, and did other fun things to fill his time. That lasted about two years, and then he grew restless. "No one prepares you," he told me, "for the day the phone stops ringing." He had always lived at a high engagement level, and he simply didn't feel vital anymore. He went back to work and now he's happy.

Look at people like Warren Buffet, Clint Eastwood, and Bob Dylan, who are doing some of the best work of their lives in their seventies and eighties. Two men I know just had their best years ever in sales, at the age of 67. We are starting to redefine the elder years from a period of being put out to pasture to one of creatively applying a lifetime of accumulated wisdom.

The old image of a gold watch, a retirement party, and a golf cart is dying. People now realize they want to remain vital, active, and contributory in their elder years. When I do financial planning with clients now it's not aimed toward a mythical retirement day, but toward a day of *financial independence*, where work becomes a choice rather than a necessity—and where the kind of work the client chooses to do is based on his values, talents, and desires.

The new retirement isn't about just burning through all the resources we saved during our working years; it's about using our financial plan to empower us to make more creative and vital choices in our later years.

Engage with the Process

Discussions about death and longevity are the hard part of financial planning. It's much more fun to talk about family reunions and cabins on the lake. We don't like to think about mortality, and we like to think about *morbidity* even less—the idea of becoming sick or disabled and a burden to our children.

But the solution is not to dismiss the issue of longevity with a nervous laugh. At some point, sooner rather than later, you *must* sit down with a planner and really engage in the process of discussing these matters. Have at least one extended and meaningful conversation with your planner, in which you make some real decisions about how you intend to live in and fund your later years.

The reason many of us are reluctant to have this conversation is that it involves picking a concrete age to plan toward. Once we do this, it changes the trajectory of our behavior. Our plan now has definite form. And the older an age we plan to live to, the tougher today's choices will become. We may need to spend less, accumulate more, and work longer. The moment we pick an age for our plan, our present behavior takes on a different significance. We might not be able to buy a new car this year; we might need to put more in our retirement account.

Tough as it might be, though, I encourage you to have this conversation earlier, rather than later. Not only will this make your goals easier to attain, but it will also help you start to see your later years as an integral part of your life—a part to embrace and look forward to, rather than deny and ignore.

6

Embrace Life Insurance and Annuities

When I sit down with clients, I encounter a lot of resistance to the idea of life insurance and annuities. Often people have read or heard something, or their parents have told them, "Never buy an annuity" or "Never buy whole life insurance." These biases stick, but the reasons behind them may be lost or forgotten.

The financial press doesn't help. Many money pundits portray whole life insurance as evil incarnate. In their minds, anyone who buys anything but term life insurance is a fool, and whole life insurance is the biggest rip-off since Bernard L. Madoff Investment Securities. On the other side of the fence are more sophisticated planners who say that the best life-insurance product, long term, is one that offers cash value, dependable payouts to your heirs, and tax advantages.

Often a client will ask me, point blank, "Mark, which is better: term or whole life insurance?" This is exactly like walking into a hardware store and asking, "Which is better: a hammer or a screwdriver?" The answer, of course, is, "It depends what you're trying to accomplish." You don't use a drill to plane wood.

Or clients might ask me, "Are annuities any good?" Insurance and annuities are not inherently good or bad products, they're just tools in the woodshop that need to be matched correctly to the job.

It's understandable why you might have some cynicism about insurance products. You've probably been sold a policy by a commissioned salesperson who presented it to you as if it were a hammer and you were a nail. That's where everything runs afoul. That's how we end up with financial products that were sold to us because the salesperson needed a commission, not because they were the best product for our needs at a particular time and place in our life.

The proper approach is to treat these products like tools. Know what each type of insurance and annuity is designed to do, understand its relative pluses and minuses, and know what your individual blueprint calls for. Your *plan* should dictate how much insurance you need, which product is most appropriate, how long you need it for, and what you can afford right now.

And then *you* should make the ultimate decision on what you'd like to purchase, not a salesperson. That's the proper way to do it. Put the horse in front of the cart, not the other way around.

Risk Management— Back to the Base of the Pyramid

The unvarnished truth is that most of us need risk management at some point in our lives. Often we need it for our entire lives, and we usually need different types at different points. As much as we may bristle at this uncomfortable fact, it's wise to own some products that transfer our risk to a third party.

Life insurance, in its simplest terms, is a product that protects your family from your dying too soon. Annuities, in essence, protect you from living too long, from outliving your assets. These vehicles cover early-life risks and late-life risks; the middle part we take care of ourselves, while we're in good health.

Let's look at each of these product types separately.

The Basics of Life Insurance

Life insurance protects us against dying too early. Statistically, this doesn't happen very often. The vast majority of us *don't* die young. But we insure this event anyway, because it would be catastrophic if it happened. So we transfer the risk.

In most cases, at least with term life insurance, the insurance company wins the bet. We, the insured, don't make a claim within the covered term, and they, the insurer, get to keep all of our money. That's why insurance companies can afford to own some of the tallest buildings in town; it's a lucrative business.

But of course, we don't really *want* to win that bet, because in order to do so, we would need to die. So, in a sense, it's a lose/lose proposition for us, which may help explain why many people have negative attitudes toward insurance companies. Still, we need to manage our risks, and insurance is the best way to do it.

Life insurance is a complex topic about which entire books could be written. Here, I'd just like to touch on some of the fundamentals.

As you probably know, there are two main types of insurance: term and permanent.

Term Life Insurance. Term life insurance, as its name implies, covers a specific term or period of years. You can buy 10-year, 15-year, 20-year, and now even 30-year term policies. The insurance has a specific death benefit and a specific term. So you might, for example, buy a $350,000 policy for a 20-year term. That means if you die within that 20-year term, your family receives $350,000, usually tax-free. If you die one day after the term expires, your family gets zero.

Term life insurance has no cash value to the insured. For that reason, term insurance is relatively inexpensive. It does its job, which is to transfer the risk of early death to another party, but it doesn't provide any other financial goodies.

Permanent Life Insurance. Permanent life insurance covers the insured for his or her whole life. When the insured dies, at any age, his or her beneficiary receives a death benefit. For this reason, permanent life insurance can be part of your estate planning. You know your beneficiaries *will* eventually get the money.

Permanent policies contain an insurance component and a savings component. As you continue to pay your premiums, the savings component slowly grows. This so-called *cash value* is your money. You can borrow against it or simply cancel your policy and take the cash (if you do this before a certain date you may need to pay a penalty). So a life policy is a true financial asset.

Life insurance policies are not the most aggressive growth vehicles on the market, but their tax benefits make them appealing in many ways. Not only is the death benefit paid out tax-free (this is true for term too), but money is also allowed to grow tax-free within the policy and can often be taken out on a tax-free basis as well. Only a Roth IRA is more tax friendly, but many high-income people earn too much to qualify for Roths.

So permanent life policies can serve as an integral part of a portfolio. Because of the cash-value aspect, however, these policies cost a great deal more than term insurance for the same death benefit.

There are three main variations of permanent life insurance: *whole life*, which usually has level premiums and benefits for the life of the policy; *universal* (or *adjustable*), in which the premium and coverage amount can be adjusted based on changing needs, and *variable*, which includes features of a tax-deferred investment fund, in that you have some control over the allocation of your money. Because the latter is tied to the market, its premiums, cash value, and benefit can go up or down.

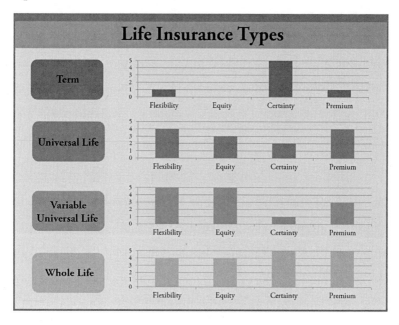

Picking the Right Tool

So as you can see, the above products are very different tools. You need the right one for the job. A simple example: You're a young executive with three kids and a mortgage. You don't have a lot of spare cash, but your family will be in big trouble if you, the breadwinner, die. Your primary need is income replacement, and plenty of it. So you should buy as much term insurance as you can afford. It's relatively inexpensive and it accomplishes its goal.

On the other hand, maybe you're a more established individual who has done well financially and whose kids may be in college. Income replacement is becoming less critical for you, and you're starting to look down the road, perhaps toward transferring the family's wealth to the next generation. You may be more interested in the cash value and liquidity aspects of a policy than the risk transfer.

It can be a big mistake to let a salesperson talk you into an investment-grade insurance policy if it's not the product that suits your needs. If you have limited cash flow and three kids at home, and you buy $100,000 of variable life insurance instead of $1 million of term insurance, that's the wrong tool for your job. We'd all like to own a Mercedes, but sometimes the Hyundai is the right car for right now.

On the other hand, you don't want to be too pennywise. The least expensive policy on the market is 10-year term insurance. But if you buy this product at age 45, that only takes you to 55. Unless you plan on dying before 55, what are you going to do next? Buy another policy? OK, but now you're adding more risk. Now you have to go through another medical exam at age 55, hope to get a good rate again, and then shoot for another 10-year policy, which will take you to 65. What if you then have diabetes? Perhaps buying something a bit longer-term, like a 30-year plan, makes more sense. These are the kinds of things an advisor who is not making a commission on selling a particular product can discuss with you.

Buy Term and Invest the Rest?

Many financial experts preach the gospel of "buy term insurance and invest the rest." The claim is that your money will work harder for you if you unbundle the death benefit from the investment component and use what you *would* have spent on the latter to buy into a mutual fund. But when you track the two scenarios—whole life vs. "term and invest"—for twenty years (assuming the same rate of return for both), what you find is that, yes, for the first three, five, maybe even nine years, the "term and invest" strategy wins out. But once you have gotten past the acquisition costs, whole life delivers better results. One primary reason is taxation. In the mutual fund world, taxes reduce your returns. In the insurance world, you're in a tax-free environment, so you have no drag on your investment earnings.

If you own a business, you may need the tool of life insurance to do jobs that go beyond income replacement. Policies can be used to fund buy/sell agreements, so that when one partner dies, the death benefit can be used to buy out their interest from their family and provide their family with cash. Life insurance can also provide key man coverage, in case someone integral to the business dies.

One tool may be used for many different jobs, but not for all jobs.

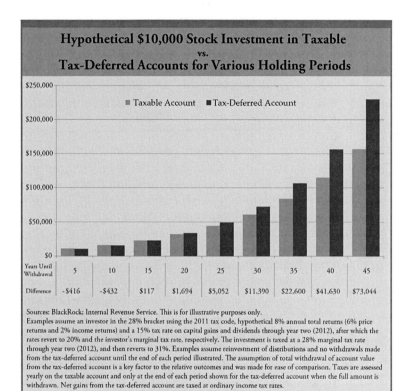

Hypothetical $10,000 Stock Investment in Taxable vs. Tax-Deferred Accounts for Various Holding Periods

Years Until Withdrawal	5	10	15	20	25	30	35	40	45
Difference	-$416	-$432	$117	$1,694	$5,052	$11,390	$22,600	$41,630	$73,044

Sources: BlackRock; Internal Revenue Service. This is for illustrative purposes only.
Examples assume an investor in the 28% bracket using the 2011 tax code, hypothetical 8% annual total returns (6% price returns and 2% income returns) and a 15% tax rate on capital gains and dividends through year two (2012), after which the rates revert to 20% and the investor's marginal tax rate, respectively. The investment is taxed at a 28% marginal tax rate through year two (2012), and reverts to 31%. Examples assume reinvestment of distributions and no withdrawals made from the tax-deferred account until the end of each period illustrated. The assumption of total withdrawal of account value from the tax-deferred account is a key factor to the relative outcomes and was made for ease of comparison. Taxes are assessed yearly on the taxable account and only at the end of each period shown for the tax-deferred account when the full amount is withdrawn. Net gains from the tax-deferred account are taxed at ordinary income tax rates.

I Won't Need Life Insurance When . . .

Another trap question I get from clients, is, "Do you need life insurance after you retire?" The client usually has a preconceived notion of what the right answer is. And if I step into that bear trap and answer the wrong way, they think, "Aha! He's trying to sell me insurance."

The truth is that most people don't *want* to drop insurance after retirement. The main reason most of us buy life insurance *initially* is income replacement. In theory, we should be able to plot the growth of both our retirement assets and our non-retirement assets and reach a point where we have enough assets and no longer need life insurance. That is what I call the "nirvana moment of life insurance." But in reality, clients never seem to reach that point.

My clients seem to dwell on two sides of an imaginary wall. On one side are those who haven't been as successful as they hoped in accumulating assets, despite their best efforts. These clients continue to need life insurance for some level of income replacement or security. This may not be their fault. Look at the people who were going to retire a couple of years prior to 2008. Suddenly there was a 35 percent drop in the stock market and their retirement assets went down by 25–35 percent. They weren't planning on owning life insurance after retirement; they thought they would be all set. But then, without warning, there was a hole to fill.

On the other side of the wall are the uber-successful clients. They've accumulated more assets than they need and their thoughts have shifted to how to preserve and transfer their wealth to the next generation, or to a charity. They discover that their life insurance can now be used to do jobs like pay federal estate taxes or help cover the costs of preserving a second home as a family compound.

Others may choose to use life insurance as a way to provide equitable distributions of wealth to their children and grandchildren. So there are all sorts of reasons to own life insurance after retirement.

The only people who really drop insurance later in life are those whose policies have become too expensive. I don't believe that in my thirty-one-year career I've ever heard, "Mark, I'm at that point where I've got enough assets and I want to cancel all my insurance." Why? Because life happens.

Second marriages, for example. Where I live, in California, these are extremely common. You do clients' planning when they're thirty-five and they have young kids in the house, and then seven years later, they're divorced and remarried and have two families to worry about. There may even be a divorce decree that requires life insurance be carried for the rest of the former couple's lives.

Or a person may have had a bout with prostate cancer, or may have lived through 2008 and 2009, and starts to think, "I don't technically *need* this insurance anymore, but I like knowing I have an extra half a million as an oops factor."

So, whether you're still in your working years or retired, it's not really a question of "Should I have insurance or not?" You want to have a combination of *different types of products* that overlap and do different things. And you don't want to put all your eggs in one basket. So maybe your blueprint says yes, your need will go down when your last child leaves the house, and then it will go down once again after college is paid for. So you can have different policies that you drop at those times. But you're not going to handle all of your insurance that way. You also want to build in an oops factor, just in case life happens, which it always does.

Annuities Also Misunderstood

Annuities are another widely misunderstood concept. If you Google "annuities," you'll get millions of hits. Simply put, annuities are vehicles that are funded up front and then pay out a stream of payments. They are often used to manage longevity risk.

The two biggest misconceptions I hear about annuities are:

1. Annuities are only distribution vehicles; they only pay out income.

2. You must give up your principle or liquidity in order to annuitize your money.

Neither of these is true.

1. **There are two types of annuity.** There are two basic types of annuity. One, which many people aren't even aware of, is designed for the accumulation of capital (with a payout later on); the other is designed strictly for distribution. The first type is called a *deferred* annuity. The owner of the annuity pays into it for a number of years and then begins to collect payments, typically in retirement. The other type is called an *immediate* annuity. In this case, the buyer pays a lump sum to the insurance company and immediately begins receiving regular payments.

Within these two categories are *fixed* and *variable* annuities. Fixed annuities pay a fixed payout for the life of the annuity; variable annuities pay an amount that's tied to the market, so the payout can go up and down.

You're probably familiar with annuities, even if you don't know it. Lifetime union pension payouts, for example, are annuity payments. An individual can also *purchase* an income stream for life. It's called *annuitization*. This is a good tool for clients who have relatively small amounts of capital but need to create as high a monthly income as possible. What you do in this situation is trade your capital to an insurance company in exchange for an income stream for life. Not only is your longevity risk transferred, but also every payment you receive is part principal and part interest, so it maximizes the amount of income that can come out.

2. **You can get income *and* liquidity.** Your father or grandfather may have told you that when you buy annuities, you always surrender your capital. Annuities *can* work that way, as described above, but there are other variations.

Today's sophisticated annuities allow you to take guaranteed income for life, *while maintaining* 100 percent liquidity. These vehicles are actually variable annuities with so-called guaranteed monthly income benefits (GMIBs)—so no matter what happens in the investment environment, your principal will go up by an interest-rate amount. These annuities allow you to take market risk, but also to have income guarantees. These are a nice fit for people who are looking for a reliable way to cover their fixed expenses during retirement.

Of course, there are always trade-offs. If you want to maximize income, you *will* need to surrender your capital and there'll be nothing left for your heirs. But if you can afford to take less income by choosing an annuity with liquidity features, then whatever is left in the annuity can be passed on to the next generation.

Compelling Reasons to Take Annuity Income

Annuities can make sense in a variety of situations. Again, it's a matter of matching the tool to the job.

For example, there's a whole industry that deals in so-called *structured settlements*. If you win a lawsuit and receive a substantial award, you might choose to have those dollars paid out in the form of a structured settlement, or annuity. Sometimes the court might order this—for example, in the case of a person who has become disabled and may need a lifetime of care. Another example is state lottery systems that give winners the option of taking either a lump sum or an annuity payment. It is well known that a large percentage of people who take lump sums are broke within five or ten years. They're just not used to managing money. So in cases where money management might be an issue, annuities can be the perfect solution.

Another situation I sometimes see is clients whose parents have modest retirement assets and may be dependent on the children for some support. The client might take the parents' assets—maybe not all of them, but a good chunk—and buy a lifetime annuity for them. This takes the pressure off the children of trying to invest that money and get above-market returns. And it provides certainty that the parents aren't going to outlive their income. The children know they are not going to get an inheritance, but they are happy to make that trade-off to ensure that their parents' basic needs are taken care of for life.

Caveat Emptor

A prospective buyer of insurance products does not have an easy job. The life insurance and annuity marketplace is crowded with people trying to sell the wrong tool for the wrong job, making misleading claims, and, in some cases, trying to sell products that are outright flawed.

Whole life insurance sellers, for example, often try to sell you whole life insurance when term would be better for you, and vice versa.

Products are often overhyped. For example, there's a product that's very popular right now called an EIA (equity indexed annuity) or just an indexed annuity. Simply explained, it's a fixed-rate annuity where, during the accumulation period, you get paid a return percentage that can go up if the stock market goes up. So if there's 10 percent market growth, you might get 5 percent. The selling point is that if the market goes down, the worst you can do is zero. Your principal is protected and you can never lose money.

Some advertisers of these products claim, "Get all the upside of the stock market with none of the down!" That's a dangerous statement, and these products are not overseen by

FINRA. The truth is that, in a market like we've been in at the time of this writing, where trading is basically sideways, these products perform very poorly. But the risks and details may not be disclosed in the ads.

As another example, I was recently with a family member who was happily sharing the fact that his annuity was earning him 10 percent. But I was familiar with the product he owned and explained to him how it worked: You put your money in, and for the first five years, you're credited with 10 percent. But the only way to get that 10 percent is to annuitize the balance at the end of five years. At that point they take your balance, divide it by ten years, and pay you out one-tenth per year. Guess what interest rate they pay you during that ten-year period? Zero. When you take the fifteen years into account that's about a 3.1 percent average return rate. Is it a bad product? Not *necessarily*, but it may not be what you thought you were getting.

Then there are some products that, in my opinion, are not good buys, period. Accidental Death and Dismemberment policies, for example. These cover things like having a safe fall on your head from a fifth-floor window. You might think, "It's pretty cheap and I can get double the death benefit for pennies on the dollar." But there's a reason for that. These events don't happen. In 31 years of paying out claims, I don't think I've ever had one person die due to a non-vehicular accident.

Another product, which is *not* cheap, is mortgage insurance. You get solicitations for this when you buy your house, but in most cases you can buy it much less expensively on your own, outside of the mortgage-insurance market.

The overall point I want to impress upon you is that life insurance and annuity products, for the most part, are not inherently good or bad. They are designed to accomplish different things. And just as you would not walk into a hardware store and buy whatever tool was in the salesperson's hand, you shouldn't buy any insurance product because the *salesperson* wants you to own it. It's about you and your needs. Period.

We all need risk-management products, but our needs are based on individual goals and circumstances. These can best be determined by going through a planning process with a trusted and product-neutral advisor. Only then can you pick the strategies and products that support what *you're* trying to accomplish. To "shop" this way takes a little more effort, but the results can make a world of difference.

7

Avoid Get-Rich-Quick or High-Risk Schemes/ Don't Go Along with the Crowd

The other day, my personal trainer—whom I like and respect—greeted me with an excited smile as I walked into the gym. "Hey, Mark," he said, "I want to run an idea by you. I know this guy, pretty sharp, and he's getting into this new investment. I was wondering what you thought about it."

I already had a bad feeling about this.

"It involves the Iraqi dinar," he continued. "Right now, no one's trading them. In fact, you can't even get your hands on them."

"Maybe that's because they're essentially worthless," I offered, trying to be helpful.

"Right, but there's a secret plan in place with the U.S. government that when they normalize relations again, these things are going to be worth a fortune. And you can only get them through this special website. They'll take as little as $1,000 as a starting investment. My guy's going in heavy, and I'm thinking of getting in too."

I exhaled briskly. I had my iPad handy and pulled up the website. A quick survey of its contents confirmed that this "investment" was flawed on every conceivable level. "Don't walk away from this deal," I told my trainer. "Run."

When I got back to the office, I met with a client to review his portfolio and was dismayed to find a recent debit of $40,000, which he hadn't discussed with me. When I asked him what he'd spent the money on, he told me it was an investment his cousin had talked him into, in a bar no less. Leaning forward, he looked me in the eye and said with conspiratorial glee, "green motorcycle technology."

I sighed. I knew it was going to be a long day.

It Happens to Everyone

It happens to all of us at one time or another. We are approached by someone we know—a friend, a relative, someone we admire or work with—who has a great investment opportunity he wants to discuss.

I find these conversations typically have two motivations. The first is that the person has made a questionable financial decision—or is *about to* make one, like my trainer—and is looking for affirmation that he did the right thing. "Oh, you've invested in a diamond mine? That sounds awesome."

The second motivation is that the person is actually trying to raise money for himself, or for someone else, toward some kind of private investment. Often the person tries to create an excited sense that this thing is spreading like wildfire. "Hey, you know, Bob is in it, and Margaret is in it, and Paula is in it." And, sure enough, you start thinking, "I don't want to be left out of this thing if everybody else is in it. What if this is the next Facebook?" Pretty soon, you're giving the idea serious thought.

As a financial advisor, I am in a unique position to see where these brother-in-law investments end up five or ten years down the road. Almost everyone's portfolio contains at least one of them—a $150,000 stake in a buddy's tequila factory that hasn't produced anything in ten years except quarterly email reports; an orange grove in Florida that a bunch of friends went in on when Florida real estate was hot; a vending-machine operation in Montreal; a New York restaurant that Johnny Depp was supposedly backing.

More than 90 percent of these investments are losers; and they often go to zero. Their common trait is that they come to us via someone we trust, respect, or like. On some level we believe that if *they're* in it, then it must be good. We become drawn in on an *emotional* level—whether that emotion is loyalty, trust, admiration, affection, or just a desire to keep family peace—rather than a logical or intellectual one. And our due diligence is shortchanged because of that emotional connection.

Unfortunately, that is a really bad way to make a decision.

The Look of the Deal

Brother-in-law investments—those deals that come to us through a personal connection—tend to share certain characteristics:

Exclusivity. There's often a "private club" or "inner circle" feeling to them. You are invited to believe that only a select few are being given this opportunity, and that it's something only insiders know about. Also, you need to act fast because the door is closing soon. This thing is a special privilege.

Coolness. Quite often, there's something inherently cool or exciting about the deal. Maybe it's a nightclub, or a new technology, or a Hollywood movie, or a resort in some exotic locale. It's something you *want* to be a part of because it will be fun to talk about with your friends and colleagues. Your personal stock will go up—you imagine—by being part of this thing.

Different this time. A story that often circulates around these investments is, "It's a different environment we're in today." The world has changed in some fundamental way and this thing represents the new wave. If you don't understand that, you are stuck in old-fashioned thinking. We saw a lot of this kind of hype when the dot-com and real-estate bubbles were blowing up.

Urgency. Very often these deals involve start-ups or a start-up mentality. There is a strong sense that we need to be "first to market." This urgency is often used as a justification for the lack of sound fundamentals, such as a good business plan, a sound management structure, and credible financials. There is often a promise that those things will come later, but for now, we've got to *move fast*.

Wacky stories. Typically, these deals have some kind of story attached to them—the wackier, the better. "So the guy who started this got stuck in an elevator with Steve Jobs before he died, and Steve told him about this new technology that was going to change the face of telecommunications . . . "

Celebrity involvement. The coup de grâce, along with the cool factor, is often that there are celebrities involved. In many cases their involvement cannot be proven, but it's fun to talk about over dinner with friends. "I'm in this thing with Tom Cruise that I'm really excited about."

These exciting qualities draw you in and make you want to become involved. But then you learn about some other traits these deals often share:

High minimums. There is often a minimum of $25,000, $50,000, or more to become involved in the investment. But while many legitimate private equity-type transactions require you to be a so-called accredited investor, many of these brother-in-law deals do not. Anyone with a checkbook and funds can get in.

Promise of liquidity, but . . . Very often these deals promise liquidity, but in fact, they are among the most illiquid investments imaginable. Once you're in, you're in. These ventures are not usually publicly traded, so there is no market for your investment if you want to sell it. Succeed or fail, you're committed till the finish. And there's a good chance you'll be asked to chip in more money down the road.

Vague on details. Often, these boutique deals provide a package of information for investors, but it doesn't go very deep. Details are vague. If you to try to probe, you are put off. That may be because the information just doesn't exist, or because, as a limited partner, you are not entitled to that information.

Poor communication. Typically, with these deals, there is a lot of communication up front, but very little later on. At the beginning, people want your money, so they wine you and dine you. They take your calls and laugh at your jokes. But once you're signed on, silence reigns. All you might receive from that point on is an annual report that essentially says, "OK, this is what we did last year," or, "We're getting ready for a public offering." You may get that same letter five or ten years in a row.

Because of the sense of personal connection you feel with the project, you are often willing to accept conditions you would not tolerate in any other deal. You become willingly blind.

Not the Right Vehicle for a Small Investor

I'm not suggesting that all brother-in-law deals are sleazy. Some *are* outright frauds, some are merely harebrained schemes, and some are legitimate, credible attempts to launch a new business. In any case, though, this type of investment might be a mismatch for a private individual doing a one-off deal.

First of all, you should know that you are probably going to be disappointed. Perhaps what attracted you to this opportunity was the idea that you were going be actively involved in something exciting. But in most cases, you soon learn that your role is a passive, backseat position. After you cut the check, your input is neither desired nor required. Tom Cruise is not calling to discuss strategy with you.

This can be especially frustrating if you are invested at a level higher than your comfort zone. When a super-wealthy celebrity throws $50,000 at a restaurant, it's no big deal; if the venture fails, it's a rounding error to him. But if $50,000 is half of your net worth, naturally you are going to want to babysit that investment. You are going to be hyper-interested in the day-to-day details. But that's exactly the opposite of what these entrepreneurs want. They don't want people calling them and emailing them and bugging them while they are trying to execute their business plan. As a result, they're unhappy, you're unhappy, and it's a mismatch.

Most small investors who get involved with a privately funded business simply do not realize how slim the odds of success are. The vast majority of these ventures fail. Maybe one in ten is successful. The odds that yours will be the one are tiny. The personal connection you feel to the investment often clouds your judgment on this. You need to realize that *any* one-off opportunity is a poor bet.

To invest successfully in new business opportunities, you need to know how to play that game, and it's a very particular game. You need to have substantial enough capital to spread around and make many, many similar investments. You need to be OK with the fact that only one in ten of your investments may come through. When you hit that occasional home run, it makes up for the failures. Conversely, the failures are the price you pay for scoring the occasional big success. To play this game successfully, you need to make this kind of investment on a regular basis and develop an eye for it; otherwise, it's probably best not to play at all.

Thirty Years to Overnight Success

Often, to lure you into these deals, one of the principals will boast of a recent huge success. But, like the gambler who never talks about all his losses, you don't see how many failed deals this person went though before scoring the big win. We all have Mark-Zuckerberg-overnight-billionaire fantasies, but the truth is that most people who make it big in any industry have been in their game a long time. I, for example, am fortunate enough to live a pretty nice lifestyle, but it took me thirty years to become a success. I've been playing my game a long time.

I once had dinner with five producers in Hollywood. I asked them, "Why is it that some really terrible movies make it to theaters and some of the best scripts never get made?" Their answer was fascinating. They talked about all the movies that *don't* get made in Hollywood. In fact, the vast majority of viable movie projects never get shot or distributed. Getting a movie made is like getting legislation through Congress, they said. It hits roadblock after roadblock, and you just have to work around these, often for five or ten *years*. Once in a while, you succeed—by dumb luck as much as by anything else—and you get the green light. At that point, your movie is *going* to get made, whether it's good or terrible. Meanwhile, great scripts fall by the wayside. That's why these producers always have a lot of projects going. Because so few make it. They're like turtle hatchlings scrambling to the sea. Movie success is not a case of overnight riches; it's a case of playing the game with dedication, year in and year out, and, occasionally, if you're lucky, being part of a blockbuster.

To expect to hit a home run with a single, one-off investment, especially as an outsider to that industry, is extremely unlikely. It does happen, but it's the exception that proves the rule.

A Windfall—Your Most Vulnerable Moment

If you have any money at all, you are vulnerable to being approached by people looking for investors. But if you receive a major windfall of some kind, that's when you are *exceptionally*

Buy My System!

Sometimes successful individuals try to sell you their systems for attaining wealth. They're basically saying, *Even though you know nothing about this industry, you can succeed by using the secrets it took me decades to learn. Take my course or purchase my software and I'll give you the inside scoop on how to* . . . make a killing as a day trader, buy real estate with no money down, exploit the Forex market for easy dollars. But think about it. There's no incentive for anyone to sell a truly successful system. If a hedge fund team, for example, developed a proprietary algorithm they used to trade successfully, there's no way in hell they would sell it to the public, thereby destroying the very edge it gives them. Often when you buy a system what you get is either (a) admission to a pyramid scheme or (b) a strategy that formerly worked but was done to death. What you virtually never get is the *current* hot strategy that is working right now. Those are not for sale.

vulnerable. That's when friends, family, and strangers come crawling out of the woodwork with potential deals. It's also a time when you are highly susceptible to making poor choices.

I was recently approached by a young client in the entertainment industry. The company she worked for had just struck a record-breaking deal with a major high-tech company, and her employers thanked her with a generous $350,000 bonus. She had never had so much money. She told me that she wanted to take $150,000 of it and invest it in a new restaurant in West L.A. The deal had all of the classic earmarks: It was a cool concept, there were celebrities involved, and it would give her something exciting and different to be involved in.

She saw this as an opportunity to have a business adventure. As a wealth manager, I saw it a little differently. What I saw was a thirty-year-old woman, who, if she invested her money wisely—using the money-doubling "rule of 72" which we'll talk about in the next chapter—could turn this $350K windfall into $4 million by the time she was 65. "If you leave this money alone," I told her, "and manage it well, it's game over for you. You've already won. Do you realize the amazing life ticket you're holding in your hand?"

Part of her did, but, being thirty, she was convinced she was going to live forever and that retirement was for people too old to have fun anymore. She was determined to do the exciting deal. So I tried to at least convince her that the $150,000 was too large a percentage of her total assets to risk on a single investment. If she was bent on doing this, I suggested she try to get in with a $50,000 or, better still, a $25,000 investment. "You're going to be a minority partner anyway. You can get the same cool factor with a lot less money on the table."

"Hey, It's Just Found Money"

I don't know if this client chose to follow my advice or not, but I was struck by something she said. When I asked why she was so determined to do the restaurant thing, she told me, "Well, this $350,000 is found money. I never planned on having it, therefore I can take huge risk with it." There is something compelling about this logic. It's also the same logic people use to blow the $2,000 they just won at the roulette wheel on the blackjack table.

I said to her, "There's a flipside to that coin. On one hand, you're right. If you lose this money, it's no big deal; you're back to where you started. On the other hand, you have a once-in-a-lifetime opportunity to build some real wealth here. You have a chance to set your future up so you can live your *whole life* with greater freedom and security. You have a chance to do some genuine good with this money, too. Maybe it's incumbent upon you to be a good steward of this money, and to protect it and grow it."

She wasn't exactly buying it, but she was listening.

"You've got an angel on one shoulder and a devil on the other," I continued. "The devil is saying, 'Go, go, go. Live for the moment.' The angel is saying, 'Wait a second; this is a blessing. Ten years from now, when you're forty years old, the restaurant will be a thing of the past, but you'll be well on your way to genuine wealth.' Think of how that will feel."

If you are lucky enough to receive a windfall, especially at a young age, don't fall into the trap of looking at it on today's cash terms only. A sum of $300,000 can translate into *millions* in the future. "Blowing" $50,000 can actually mean blowing $600,000, when you factor in the money's future growth potential. So think about that before you sink $35,000 into your neighbor's new bar. I'm not saying never take a risk,

I'm saying understand the type of potential loss you're *really* looking at. It changes your perspective a little.

What to Do When Your Brother-in-Law Comes Knocking

So what should you do on that fateful day when your brother-in-law shows up at your door with a computer-printed investment brochure and a six-pack of microbrew, wanting to talk? Here are a few thoughts:

Let your advisor or CPA play the "bad cop." I have a client who is quite wealthy and also a very nice person. Many people ask her for her time, and she gives it generously. They try to get her to invest in things. The approach she and I have worked out is that whenever she gets into these situations, she listens politely, then says, "I don't do anything unless my financial advisor approves it, so I have to run it by him first." There's no way a reasonable person can object to this. This gets her out of the hot seat, plus it gives her another set of eyes to look at the deal. It's always a good idea to tell people there's someone else who needs to weigh in.

Do your due diligence. When a person you trust and admire tells you about a rare investment opportunity, it can be tempting to throw your critical faculties out the window and become a true believer. But first you need to do some digging. Don't be mesmerized by the positive aspects of the deal; go looking for the negatives. Find out what losing projects this team has been involved with and why they didn't work. Notice what people are *not* saying. Remember, sins of omission can be just as deceitful as outright fraud. Shine a light on all of the details. If the investment is good, it will stand up to the scrutiny. But if you start hearing things like, "We don't really have audited financials yet," take that as a red flag.

Invest only an amount you can afford to lose. We've talked about this before, but it bears repeating. Make sure any money you decide to invest comes only from the top of your financial pyramid. These deals are speculative in nature, no matter who presents them to you. You should never invest more than you are comfortable losing—not only financially, but emotionally. If you succumb to the temptation to invest more than you should, not only are your finances at stake, but so are your relationships. And you can't put a price on those.

As a wealth manager, I'm in a bit of a no-win situation when it comes to advising clients about brother-in-law projects. If I say, "Don't invest," and I'm right, the client may never even realize it. If I say, "Don't invest," and I'm wrong, then I'm really in trouble. The client could have had a big win and I talked her out of it. If I say no too often, I run the risk of being fired by the client. Even *I* must admit to losing patience with CPAs and planners who habitually say no to every investment idea. They know that a "no" is safe and you can never go catastrophically wrong with a "no," so they negate every idea. That's not the right attitude either.

Occasionally, a good investment *will* present itself, but you should always recognize that the odds are against it. With that in mind, be objective, get a second opinion, and do your due diligence. If, after careful consideration, you decide to say yes, then let the money go, with no expectations. If it pays off, consider it gravy. If it doesn't, well then, consider it an investment in your family relationships.

8

Start Now and Reap the Rewards Later

"I'll begin a diet when the New Year rolls around."

"I'll quit drinking tomorrow."

"I'm going to start calling my mom once a week."

"Honey, we ought to get working on that living will."

"One of these days, I'm going to put together a new resume and start testing the job market."

We human beings are of two minds. Part of us knows what we *should* do; the other part of us resists making change. Change is too much work. It's uncomfortable. It's disruptive. It's risky. So instead of making a change, we do the next best thing: We talk about it. We put it off until tomorrow. We procrastinate.

One of the all-time favorites on the procrastination list is, "I'm going to start my financial planning . . . any day now." But somehow, the stars never seem to align. And so we go on, day after day, year after year, failing to make a meaningful financial plan and hoping that everything will spontaneously work out for the best.

Just as a physician witnesses the results of thirty years' worth of "I'll quit smoking tomorrow," a financial advisor witnesses the results of thirty years' worth of "I'll start planning tomorrow." I want you to know that there is *so much good* you can accomplish by making the decision earlier in adulthood rather than later. And there is so much opportunity you miss out on by procrastinating.

Why Do We Procrastinate around Planning?

There are some specific reasons, I think, why we tend to put off financial planning even more than other worthy goals.

Feeling overwhelmed. The idea of putting together a plan can seem staggering. First, you have to pull together all of your financial records and review them. Then, you need to find a professional you want to work with or a website or software you're going to use, and you don't know where to start. You need to input a boatload of data and maybe learn new terms. You need to have difficult conversations with your spouse. When we humans get overwhelmed, we often opt for doing nothing.

Embarrassment. Embarrassment is a huge factor. Studies have shown that many people would rather die than be seriously embarrassed. And money brings up a *lot* of shame—shame that you don't have better knowledge of financial matters, shame about the lack of assets you've been able to accumulate at your age, shame over foolish financial decisions—or *non-*decisions—you've made in the past.

Fear of loss of control. Maybe you feel that if you go to a planner, you will need to give up control of your finances to someone else, and you're not comfortable with that. You know you haven't been managing your money brilliantly, but you *have* developed a system you're comfortable with, and you don't want to do things differently. You *like* your color-coded file folders.

Lack of perceived need. Many people harbor the unspoken belief that "someone else will take of me when I get older." This feeling is particularly prevalent amongst millennials (though certainly not exclusive to them). Today, it's common for young adults to remain dependent on their parents throughout much of their twenties and even into their thirties. There's a general lack of urgency about assuming ownership of one's future.

On a related note, some people are just naturally optimistic. They have a cheerful belief that "the universe will provide," so planning isn't really necessary.

Addiction to instant gratification. There's also the fact that our culture has lost patience with anything that takes time to develop. We all want instantaneous results. We have Netflix and DVRs because we can't even stand sitting through TV commercials anymore, and we lose our patience if a text or an email takes more than an instant to reach its target. Even financial trading has become a push-button affair. High-speed trading is what moves the markets now.

Along with this impatience, we've developed a "have it now" mentality. Why drive a Ford when finance rates allow you to drive a Mercedes? Instead of saving for the future, we want to have the good things now and put them on a tab.

Lack of marketing and resources. Finally, there is an issue for which my industry is partially responsible. And that's the systemic lack of financial services for the middle market. Most financial advisors market to, and work with, only the upper market. The reason is obvious: That's the group that can afford to pay our fees. Meanwhile, there are horrible statistics on the middle market owning life insurance and taking other basic planning steps. These people are falling through the cracks. It's hard to do financial planning when services don't seem to be available to you.

The Cost of Procrastinating

So there are many powerful forces working against financial planning these days. It's no surprise that people are putting it off. This would not be a problem, except for the fact that *waiting has a serious cost.*

Going back to our health analogy, the more years you smoke cigarettes, eat fatty foods, and treat the treadmill as if it were a communicable disease, the worse the consequences for your long-term health. Of course, it always pays to start taking care of your health, no matter how old you are, but if you start when you are fifty-five instead of twenty-five, a certain amount of damage has already been done. You have to work harder to get results, and the benefits you receive are more limited.

There are two main costs to putting off financial planning. One is loss of accumulation. Let's call that an opportunity cost; we'll talk about that in a minute.

The other cost is risk. Most people who do delay their financial planning are unknowingly exposing themselves to prolonged risk, but they don't know it because no one has pointed it out to them. Let's look at risk first.

Risk

One of the early steps I take with clients when we sit down to do financial planning is risk analysis—the bottom part of the pyramid. What I frequently discover is that people are carrying huge amounts of risk that they aren't aware of.

For example, a professional person or entrepreneur has an enormous risk for litigation. And I don't mean just for malpractice-type issues; I mean for asset seizure. One thing that can happen, for example, is that someone in your family has a car accident and there are high damage claims or medical claims. The attorneys for the other party discover that your personal assets aren't high enough, so they come after your business assets. Happens all the time.

One of the easiest things you can do to address this is to own an umbrella policy with high limits. An umbrella policy extends the coverages on your auto and liability insurance. I can't tell you how many people have never heard of umbrella insurance and are completely unaware of their exposure. Until they sit down with a planner.

Another risk of delaying planning is that your estate documents may not be done, or done properly. This is not just a financial issue; it's a *life* issue. In the absence of a will, you may be putting your family at risk. One of the purposes of a will, for instance, is to select guardians for the minor children. These are the people who will raise your children in your absence. If you don't have a will, your kids could end up with whatever relative a judge decides is best.

You are probably running risks in the life-insurance arena as well. You may not be carrying enough coverage because no one has ever done an analysis with you.

You may also be carrying bad investments, risky investments, or poorly diversified investments. You may be spending too much money, carrying too much high-interest credit card debt, or maintaining too little liquidity.

You don't know any of these things because no one has told you.

And remember, it's the nature of risks that they tend to magnify over time. Here's a simple example: If you leave a board loose on a staircase for one day, odds are that no one will get hurt, but if you leave that board loose for months or years, someone will almost certainly have a fall eventually.

That's the way time affects risk. By delaying making a financial plan for years, or decades, you may be turning small risks into large ones.

Opportunity Cost

Lost earnings are an enormous cost of procrastination. Most people do not begin a serious, dedicated savings plan until they do some financial planning. And failure to start saving at an early age is probably the greatest financial tragedy I see in my work. It's a tragedy because when people *do* start saving early, their money does truly astonishing things for them, thanks to the power of compounding.

Albert Einstein is said to have called compounding the eighth wonder of the world. If he didn't really say it, he should have. Compounding is a magical thing.

When money is allowed to compound, it grows at an ever-accelerating rate. It starts out growing slowly and steadily, then, after a number of years, it begins to multiply crazily. I recently read that Warren Buffett made more than 90 percent of his wealth after age 60. At age 60 he was worth $3.8 billion; when he turned 85, he was worth $58.5 billion, largely through the engine of compounding.[8]

You probably know what compounding is, but let's do a quick review. The simplest definition is *gaining earnings on*

---

8 http://www.thestar.com/business/personal_finance/spending_saving/2014/12/11/start_saving_young_and_watch_small_amounts_grow_mayers.html

earnings. The way it works is that you continually add whatever returns your money is earning back into the pool, so that you continue to get returns not only on the original principal, but also on the amount you keep adding back in.

Let's say you have $1,000 and you invest it at a generous 10 percent return rate. After a year, you will have gained $100. You put that $100 back into the pool. Now you have $1,100. You continue to invest for a second year at 10 percent. For year two, you earn $110 because the total you invested was larger than in the first year. Again, you take those earnings and plow them back into the pool. Your new total is $1210. For year three, your earnings are $121. And so on. The money is working for you without your doing a thing.

Time is the critical factor here. The longer you allow money to compound, the more steeply its increase rate goes up. Money invested at 6 percent will double in twelve years, but will quadruple in twenty-four years. Money that is left to compound for thirty, forty, fifty, or more years begins to produce incredible earnings. And the best part is, you don't have to lift finger, or even add any more money in. (But, of course, if you *do* keep adding to the account, your earnings get turbocharged.)

When thinking about compounding, the "rule of 72" can be used to estimate how long it will take your money to double. You simply divide 72 by the interest rate your money is earning. So let's say your money is earning 7 percent, an achievable long-term rate. Dividing 72 by 7 gives you 10.3. It will take roughly ten years for your money to double.

What you need to realize is that a human lifespan gives you only so many doubles. So if you start investing/saving when you're young, you can get one, two, even three more doubles than those who start later.

The point is that if you are a half-decent accumulator, and you start saving right out of college, your success is basically *assured*. You won't have to work at it or worry about it. Your finances will take care of themselves. If you don't start early, there's a hefty price for waiting. At a 7 percent interest rate, you lose a doubling round for every ten years you delay starting. That's huge. If you invested $25,000 at age twenty, you would have roughly $800,000 in your account at age seventy. If you

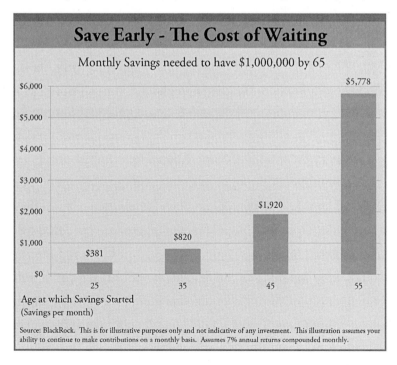

133

started at age thirty, *with the same $25,000*, you would have only $400,000 at retirement time. If you waited till age forty to invest the same amount, you would have only $200,000. It's those later doublings that work the real magic. And those occur only if you start early.

That's the true hidden price of procrastination.

A Planner Can Show You Consequences

If you understand the way money grows through compounding, you start to realize that every financial decision you make in your life has consequences down the road, in terms of the potential cost of lost opportunity. Most of us prefer not to think about this. We want to spend our money the way we want. But that's why it's so important to talk to a planner—the earlier, the better. A planner—at least one who works as I do—won't tell you how to spend your own money. But she or he can point out the opportunity costs, based on your own financial goals, so that you have a fuller perspective on your actions.

Think of a simple decision like an automobile purchase. Let's say you're thirty years old and you've just gotten your first big bonus. You decide it's time to buy yourself a luxury import. But it costs $30,000 more than a nice domestic car. You give your planner a ring, and he reminds you of the goals you stated when making your financial plan. He points out that this $30,000, if invested in your retirement account instead, will be worth nearly half a million dollars by the time you're seventy (keep in mind, the assumed rate of return is 7 percent annual). That's your vacation home in the mountains, paid for in cash! You may still decide to buy the import car, but now you will know the true price you're paying for it. It sure puts a different spin on instant gratification.

Or think about shopping for a home for your young family. You might find two homes of comparable size and quality, but one is in a more prestigious ZIP code. It will mean an additional $425 in monthly mortgage payments, or about $5,000 annually. What if you realized that you could invest that extra $5,000 a year and, by doing so, take care of your kids' college educations, free and clear?

By sitting down with an advisor, early in your adult life, and getting your important goals down on paper, you create a compass by which you can now make all future decisions. When you're weighing big purchases or other financial choices, your plan can remind you of the goals you said were important. But in the absence of a plan you're committed to, you have no real context for making money decisions and no concrete reason not to indulge your every financial whim.

I often hear clients say, "I wish I had known you back then. I might've made a different choice."

Some Other Reasons to Start Planning Now

There are some other compelling reasons to put financial planning on your agenda sooner rather than later. We talked about some of the major reasons in an earlier chapter—things like the improved success rate you achieve by writing goals down, the value of having an accountability partner, and the benefits of working with an ally who can cheer you on and help you stay the course in stormy waters.

Here are some even more specific ways that planning can help. Again, time is a major factor. The earlier you meet with a planner, the more cumulative benefits you receive and the less lifetime risk you take on.

You root out duplication and lower your costs. When you sit down with a planner, he or she will often find duplication and overlap in your insurance policies and other areas. Fixing these will save you money.

You can also save money in the investment area. A lot of hidden fees and costs are embedded within investment products, such as mutual funds and annuities. The average consumer is not even aware that he or she is paying these fees. A smart and knowledgeable planner can streamline your portfolio to help get rid of duplication and hidden costs. Every year you *delay* seeing a planner, on the other hand, may be another year you're throwing money away.

Your i's get dotted and your t's get crossed. Another great benefit of planning is that you get your tax and legal work done. It is shocking how many people—especially high-net-worth individuals—do not have even basic wills. There's a perception that wealthy people have their legal acts together, but nothing could be further from the truth. In fact, many wealthy people have layers of gatekeepers around them, which means they don't have anyone marketing services to them or reminding them about things they should be doing. So they might have a will, but it might be twenty years old and not even have their children's names on it.

Very often clients have outgrown their tax preparer, too, but don't realize it. For various reasons, they may need to move up to a medium- or large-sized accounting firm. Sitting down with a planner can help you to identify such needs.

You start your generational planning. Meeting with a planner also gets the generation-planning ball rolling, often for the first time. How much do you want the children to inherit? Are they going to work in the family business? What about the grandkids? Most clients I meet do not begin to think seriously about generational planning until the day they sit down to make a written financial plan.

Overcoming Resistance

It's easy to go on, month after month, year after year, *planning* to make a plan, but not really getting around to it. After all, making a plan is far less enjoyable than buying a new flat-screen TV. I don't know anyone whose endorphins get fired off by putting money in a 401(k) or buying life insurance.

I think the key is to start small. That can mean just getting organized. Open an Excel spreadsheet and enter your assets. List the name of the asset—401(k), cash in the bank, mutual fund, 529 plan—on the left side, the amount it contains on the right side, and the date at the top. Then promise yourself that every month you're going to redo the numbers and add it all up again. This act alone has amazing power. It's also a good step to take for your family, because now if something should happen to you, you have all of your assets listed together in one place.

Start investing, too, even if it's only a tiny amount. Most mutual funds will allow you to invest as little as $25 a month. When I was just a teenager, my dad started me in Templeton World Fund at $25 a month. And I stuck with it. Every month I put that money in—when I worked part time, when I went to college. By the time I rolled that account over, many years later, it had thousands upon thousands of dollars in it. It's a growing part of my estate to this day.

And for Heaven's sake, if you are not putting money in your company's 401(k), start immediately. Perhaps you have convinced yourself—especially if you are a young person with a lot of expenses and tight resources—that you can't afford a 401(k) contribution. I strongly encourage you to rethink that logic, especially if your employer has any kind of matching program. By not participating in that program, you are literally throwing money away. You *must* find the money to participate, no matter what scrimping you need to do. If you're not doing that, you're missing the boat. Plain and simple.

Saving and investing is like a muscle. You need to exercise it. And the more you do, the stronger the muscle grows. You start out small and then pretty soon, you start to see results.

It feels good. And that makes you want to save more. The rewarding feeling you get from seeing your money grow begins to feel better than the superficial buzz you get from buying a new living room set.

In the end, it's the *act* of exercising the muscle that matters far more than whatever particular method you are using. People who show up at the gym five times a week get stronger, whether they're doing Pilates, free weights, Nautilus, or an aerobics class. Whether you're saving/investing $100 a month, $10,000 a month, or $100,000 a month—and whether you're putting that money into a 401(k), a taxable brokerage account, or a mutual fund—you're exercising that muscle. I can tell you, looking back on thirty-one years of practice, that the difference between those who do well financially and those who don't is the exercising of that muscle on a regular basis, in good years and bad. It's not so much the quality of the investments or the size of the return rate; it's the exercising of the muscle.

The earlier you start, the better. So stop procrastinating and make a plan!

9

Find the Right Advisor For Your Needs

Feeling overwhelmed, as I mentioned, is a big reason why people delay seeking out financial planning. The industry does little to help with this. The world of professional financial services can be stunningly confusing. The average person who turns to the Yellow Pages or does an online search for financial services is often assaulted by a barrage of alphabet soup—CFA, IAR, CFP, CLU, ChFC, LIFA—and jargon salad: fiduciary, custodian, planner, broker—that threatens to wash away all hope for clarity. And sanity.

The confusion has only increased in the modern era. Many years ago, before regulations changed in the wake of

Alphabet Soup of Professional Financial Designations	
Acronym	**Designation**
AIF	Accredited Investment Fiduciary
CFA	Chartered Financial Analyst
CFP	Certified Financial Planner
CFS	Certified Fund Specialist
ChFC	Chartered Financial Consultant
CIC	Chartered Investment Counselor
CIMA	Certified Investment Management Analyst
CLU	Chartered Life Underwriter
CMT	Chartered Market Technician
CPA/PFS	Certified Public Accountant/Personal Financial Specialist
CPWA	Certified Private Wealth Advisor
CRC	Certified Retirement Counselor
MBA	Masters in Business Administration
MFP	Master Financial Planner

*FINRA.org has listed over 160 professional designations

the Glass-Steagall Act, banking, insurance, and investing were separate industries. It was fairly easy to understand what people's jobs were. Nowadays, everybody does a bit of everything, and it's very difficult to determine who does what, and, more importantly, who does what competently.

Even at my own firm, for example, we have four external parties we're associated with: a custodial firm, a broker dealer, an insurance agency, and a registered investment advisory firm. So my clients get a statement with all of these firms' names on it. What do they all mean? Why so many players?

To the untrained person, everyone starts to look and sound the same.

Rather than try to offer an exhaustive—and probably boring—breakdown of all the roles within the financial-services industry, let's just look at it from one angle. Let's assume you're looking for a general advisor who will review your overall finances and sit down to make a comprehensive plan with you.

In order to find this person, there are some helpful distinctions you will want to be aware of. All financial advisors are *not* the same.

Advisor vs. Salesperson (Process vs. Product)

One of the most important differentiators to consider, when looking at an advisor, is whether the person is a true advisor or a salesperson. Very often, one masquerades as the other. Understanding a professional's motivation is vital in making a good decision.

Some finance professionals make their money by selling financial products; others are product-neutral. The former may sit down with you and offer general financial advice, but their ultimate goal—the way they make their living—is to sell products and earn commissions. If someone is an annuities salesperson, let's face it, he's going to talk to you about annuities and why you should own them. All conversational roads will lead back to annuities.

Generally speaking, if an advisor works under the auspices of a company that sells proprietary financial products, he or she will try to sell you that company's products.

The fact that someone is a salesperson is not necessarily bad. A highly skilled salesperson offering quality products or services can be of great value, provided those are the products you truly need, based on a sound financial plan.

A pure advisor is more *process*-based than product-based. His or her job is to lead you through a process to help you determine what products, if any, you need, and what strategies you should be employing to reach your financial goals. Process-based advisors can be regarded as true third parties, because theoretically, they're not driven by commissions. Therefore, the strategies, concepts, and products they recommend should be unbiased.

Big Firm vs. Boutique

Another important distinction to note is "large institution vs. independent advisor." Some people like big institutions. They are comforted by working under the auspices of a large brand. Every bank now has its own insurance arm and investment arm, so you can often get your financial services at the same place you do your banking. Under this scenario, though—again—you're typically going to be sold name-brand products, which may or may not be best in class. There are some larger advising firms that are not product-affiliated.

The opposite of the big firm is what is known as the boutique firm. Boutiques have fewer built-in conflicts of interest, because they're not associated with proprietary products and services. They also tend to be more nimble. They don't have the same institutional pressures, and they're free to be creative and do whatever is best for the client. (Of course, as president and owner of a boutique firm, I am a bit biased.) Boutiques tend to be more niche-based in the clients they serve.

With a boutique, very often, you, the client, deal directly with the business owner or primary decision maker. With a big firm, the person you deal with directly is probably not the person making the investment decisions; those are handled by someone back in Philadelphia or New York. Your agent is really just in charge of the relationship with you. More likely than not, this person will be replaced in six months or a year, so there will be a bit of a revolving door.

A boutique, on the other hand, can maintain long-term personal relationships with its clients; I've been seeing some of my clients for thirty years. Of course, there is a flip side to this: If your advisor gets hit by a bus, what will happen? Will you be left "orphaned" and without services? A boutique firm should have a good continuity plan in place for its clients.

Comprehensive vs. Silo

Another consideration when vetting a financial advising firm is, "Are you a comprehensive agency?" A comprehensive advisor is someone who will look at all of your financial needs, all of your goals and objectives, and all of the different buckets of money you need to allocate for various purposes.

On the other side of the aisle are what I call "silo" operators. These are companies that specialize or focus on only one aspect of financial planning. Some firms invest only for college funding, for example; others might handle only retirement money—401(k)s and IRAs. Good silo firms are completely up front about the kinds of service they specialize in, and many of these firms are very good at what they do. Individuals and companies use silo firms to accomplish particular financial goals.

There are also firms that specialize according to their training, skill set, or orientation. An investment-oriented firm might look at all of your goals, but might focus only (or mainly) on investing your money well. They may not help you with risk-management needs, such as life insurance. Their focus is entirely on the returns side of the equation.

It's fine to work with a silo firm, provided you know that's what you're doing, and you're doing it intentionally. The problem is that some firms are not sufficiently clear about the fact that they are offering narrow services. The inexperienced client thinks he is getting overall financial advice, but he is really getting help with only one aspect of his financial needs. The firm, for its part, may have no interest in enlightening the client.

This is a situation I see frequently. Clients go out into the financial-services world seeking comprehensive financial advice and think that's what they're getting, but what they're really getting is a silo or product-driven approach of some kind. They end up with three large whole life insurance policies. Or with a stockbroker who gets them into all mutual fund portfolios.

Or perhaps they sit down with a planner who tailors a great retirement plan for them, but who doesn't do anything to help them buy a house or pay off their student loans. No one is asking them, "What happens if you die too early, live too long, or become disabled?" The client is being duped, either intentionally or passively, by virtue of the fact that he believes he is receiving comprehensive advice, when, in fact, he is not.

Six months later, the dissatisfied client seeks me out, armed with a portfolio that's woefully full of holes. So we have to start from square one. Only now, he has a chip on his shoulder. He may have been saddled with heavy commission fees that can't be unwound. He feels as if he has been sold a bill of goods, so his attitude toward me is wary. There's not necessarily anything wrong with the products or services he's bought, but these products were not sold to him as part of an intelligently designed, customized plan, so they don't make sense as a whole.

The silo approach is not wrong, by any means. In fact, when it comes to large or complex estates (and businesses), it often does make sense to hire specialized silo firms. But of course, you still need a coordinator or "CEO" to pull it all together. This is how wealthy families sometimes operate. A CEO is placed in charge of the family office and hires silo firms to manage the moving parts.

But for the average person, with a fairly simple estate, a comprehensive and well-rounded advisor is probably the best choice. If you need extra depth in one particular area, your advisor can always outsource for that. A comprehensive advisor can take a global, holistic look at your finances and help you put together a total package that works for all of your goals and needs.

Some Questions to Ask

So those are a few of the major distinctions that can help you sort out one advisement firm from another. There are also several questions I recommend asking. These can help you narrow the field even more and eliminate firms that aren't a good fit.

May I see your resume?

One of the first things you should do when screening an advisor or group is look at their resume. Ask if they have any conflicts of interest—for example, are they affiliated with a parent company whose products they sell? Or are there areas of financial planning they don't address, such as risk management? Ask if they do comprehensive planning—i.e., if they will actually put a plan together or just smile at you as they hand you your new product package. Also ask about any legal issues or major complaints they've had. Is there anything that might show up on a FINRA (Financial Industry Regulatory Authority) search? (You can check this yourself at brokercheck.finra.org.)

As for licenses, the main things to look for in a well-rounded advisor are FINRA registration, licensure to sell insurance and annuity products, and some kind of securities registration, such as Series 7 or Series 63, as well as proof of competency to provide advisory services (Series 65 or 66/IAR registration). Someone who is licensed only on the securities side or only on the insurance side probably will not be able to make a comprehensive, unbiased plan with you.

It's important to know that while licensure is essential, "credentials" are not always what they appear to be. A financial-planning certification, such as CFP, is fine, but some of the smartest and best advisors don't have many credentials at all. On the other hand, there are many impressive-sounding titles one can acquire simply by taking a two-hour course online; these are not especially robust or meaningful, but they look good in a frame on the wall.

How do you get paid?

A telling differentiator among advisors is the way they get paid. There are two main ways advisors make money. They are either fee-based or commission-based. A commission-based advisor makes money from selling financial products, or, in the case of a stockbroker, making trades. These people basically fall into the salesperson mold.

A fee-based advisor works for either an asset-based or service-based fee. The asset-based approach is more common. The advisor's fee is based on a percentage of the assets she handles for the client. Some advisors also work on an hourly fee basis or on price-per-service model. They might charge, for example, a flat fee of $2,500 to create a financial plan.

Fee-based advisors' income is not generally tied to selling clients any particular product. This means, theoretically, that they don't have inherent conflicts of interest. An advisor may sometimes use a combination of these payment methods, and that's fine, provided he discloses this to clients.

There are also performance fees, whereby an advisor takes a percentage of the upside. This form of compensation is highly regulated and associated mostly with hedge funds. You won't see it too often.

Advising fees can seem high, but sometimes when a trained advisor roots out all the embedded fees that you're already paying in mutual funds and other products, your overall fees can actually go down.

Are you a custodial firm?

One of the big red flags to watch out for in the financial-advisement industry is a firm that serves as its own asset custodian.

In the finance world, custody refers to the physical, contractual control of the underlying securities. In the old days, when you bought a stock, you got a stock certificate and placed it in your safe. Today, everything is done electronically. There are companies, such as Schwab, TD Ameritrade, and Pershing, whose role as custodian is to hold money and securities. They are designated third parties, meaning, they don't push for other products.

An advisory firm should have the ability to move money, but it should never actually hold the money. Dividing these roles creates a checks-and-balances system. Every month, the custodian issues statements to the investor. That way, you know someone is watching the store.

The reason Bernie Madoff was able to get away with what he did for so long—besides the fact that people wanted to believe he was working money miracles—was that he served as his own custodian. He made up his own statements, which, over time, became exercises in creative writing. Checks were made out directly to him; there was no oversight.

Custody is a very big deal. Never, never, never should the manager and the custodian be one and the same.

Do you have discretion?

Asking about discretion is another way to hone in on an advisor who's the right fit. Discretion means that your advisor has the ability to move money without your specific acknowledgement or consent. When you sign a contract granting discretion, you are essentially saying, "I agree to your investment philosophy. I trust you to do your thing." The manager is free to take creative control of the investment process, buying and selling as he sees fit. You're essentially along for the ride.

Many firms don't have discretion by choice. That means every move made must be approved by the client. These firms don't buy, sell, or alter anything without a client's specific consent, either verbal or written.

Arguments can be made on either side of the discretion fence. It really comes down to what you're comfortable with.

But you should give this issue some thought before you sign on with an advisor. Are you comfortable surrendering complete control or do you prefer to have approval at each decision-making juncture?

Are you a fiduciary?

Whether or not an advisor has fiduciary responsibility is another important consideration. Not all advisors do. For example, an insurance broker who's also registered to sell securities has only the responsibility to make sure that you're "suitable" for an investment—that your basic financial circumstances indicate you're an appropriate buyer. This is very different from a fiduciary level of care, which is the highest level of care under the law. A fiduciary is obligated to do what is in your best interests, considering all the facts and circumstances. When you work with a registered investment advisory firm, you receive a fiduciary level of care.

If you can get this extra level of care and watchfulness for no extra cost—and you can—why wouldn't you?

Who's your ideal client?

Most advisors specialize. Typically, this breaks down along the lines of either the type of service they provide or the type of client they serve. Some advisors only design and manage 401(k)s. Some advisors work mainly with retirees, or with high-net-worth entrepreneurs, or with the employees of companies. Most advisors have an ideal client they prefer to work with, which is why they have investment minimums. This allows them to be selective about their clientele.

You're better off working with a firm where you're a member of the target niche they serve.

So ask a prospective advisor questions like:

- What's your minimum?

- Who do you work with?

- What's your niche?

- What does your ideal client look like?

The firm might occasionally work with people outside their niche, but in that case, you're probably not getting their best work, because it's not their specialty.

Do you provide an IPS?

Look for an advisor who provides an IPS, or Investment Policy Statement. An IPS is a document that outlines the agreed-upon allocation for your money. It stipulates things like time horizons for investments and the acceptable portfolio mix within specified parameters. You agree on all these "rules of the road" for the handling of your money, and then both you and your advisor sign the IPS. A copy is provided to you, and every year it's updated.

An IPS helps prevent communication miscues between you and your advisor. IPSs have been used with institutions forever—they're standard operating procedure—but for smaller customers, this is not always the case.

Some Things to Watch out For

There are also some red flags to watch for when shopping for a high-quality, client-centered advisor. I've mentioned a few of these already. One obvious red flag, for example, is a claim or suggestion by an advisory firm that they can help you get market-beating returns. Not only is beating the market unrealistic on a long-term basis, it is not even the goal of a comprehensive financial advisor. Another flag—a yellow one, if not a red one—is the silo-type or product-based firm masquerading as a comprehensive one. Here are a few others:

Failure to listen. I hear nightmare stories about advisors who just don't listen to clients or pay attention to their needs. They offer a square hole and, even if you're a round peg, they're going to hammer you into it. For example, they might have a certain perspective on risk, and even if you say, "I'm not comfortable with this," they put you in the risky vehicle anyway. If you pick up any signs that an advisor is not really listening to you during the interview stage, you can be pretty certain he won't listen to you once he has your money.

Failure to communicate. Many advisors are quite chatty and solicitous with new clients during the honeymoon period, but then, once the client is signed, the client hardly every hears from them. Read some online reviews to see if your prospective advisor has a history of communication complaints. Look for an advisor who has a system in place for meeting in person with you, or at least communicating by phone. It should be important to the advisor that meetings and calls occur regularly.

Flashy promises. While a good money manager should be successful financially—you probably don't want to work with someone who's living at the Y and driving a '93 Chevy Cavalier—be wary of those who are all about showiness and braggadocio. "Hey, I'm getting 14 percent on this investment, why don't you join me?" It seems every month I hear about some new money manager who's gone belly up, either by perpetrating outright fraud or becoming too enthusiastic about some new financial vehicle (typically involving real estate). I mentioned second trust deeds, for example, in an earlier chapter. These were great and then suddenly, they weren't. It wasn't until the real estate market tanked that buyers finally read the small print: If this thing goes under, you get zero.

A flashy manager who will take as much money as you'll give him and place it in unproven, unregistered vehicles ought to be avoided like a scorpion's stinger.

Hedge funds. Finally, I recommend being cautious about advisors that steer you toward hedge funds. Hedge funds are private vehicles that are typically available only to higher-net-worth investors. Theoretically, they provide better value in the form of long-term returns, but that is yet to be proven. Hedge funds are unregulated to a great extent and have very high fee structures.

Many of the finance world's best and brightest work in hedge funds. Thus far, though, their returns over time have not been demonstrably better than those of traditional fund managers. And when hedge funds go bad, they go really bad. Some institutions may use hedge funds effectively, as part of their long-term diversification strategies, but the average investor needn't get involved with them.

Give It a Rethink

Perhaps you can see now that advisors vary greatly. If you've been using "All those advisors are the same" as your financial mantra, you might want to reconsider that position. Unless you're a very savvy DIY type, you are probably selling yourself short by not working with an advisor.

Studies have shown, for instance, that the average return for a small investor working without an advisor is around 2 percent. What's the explanation for this? People buy at exactly the wrong time and sell at exactly the wrong time. They make decisions emotionally, but justify them rationally.

The year 2008 was a great example of this. I and other advisors had to field daily phone calls from clients who were panicking and didn't know what to do. Despite our own emotions, we told our clients, "You need to calm down." People who had good relationships with their advisors during that period had far better ultimate results than those whose only compass was their emotions. Investors who stayed in the market through 2008 saw their investment dollars come back and had great returns in the years that followed. Many lone-wolf investors did not.

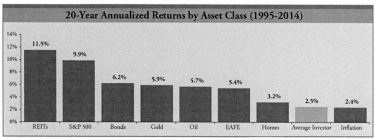

Source: J.P. Morgan Asset Management, Dalbar Inc. Indexes used are as follows: REITS: NAREIT Equity REIT Index, EAFE: MSCI EAFE, Oil: WTI Index, Bonds: Barclays Capital U.S. Aggregate Index, Homes: median sale price of existing single-family homes, Gold: USD/troy oz, Inflation: CPI. Average asset allocation investor return is based on an analysis by Dalbar Inc., which utilizes the net of aggregate mutual fund sales, redemptions and exchanges each month as a measure of investor behavior. Returns are annualized (and total return where applicable) and represent the 20-year period ending 12/31/14 to match Dalbar's most recent analysis.

A good advisor has a great deal of wisdom and insight that the average person does not possess. An advisor also has an opinion, a point of view, a way of putting the market news of the day into meaningful perspective. An individual working alone, in a DIY fashion, often has no context in which to make decisions and so becomes highly vulnerable to whatever the hysteria *du jour* might be.

10

Creating a Positive Legacy

"**H**mm, maybe if I procrastinate long enough in getting my financial act together, I won't have to do it at all! I'll die and it will be my family's problem."

I don't think many people *consciously* entertain such thoughts (unless they really dislike their families), but I do think a lot of us passively allow our finances to drift in that direction. We know we *should* be cleaning up our messes, but it always seems like a task we can get around to later. Too often, later becomes *too* late. I have seen countless disasters—often in wealthy and responsible families—brought on by loving, well-intentioned people who never got around to organizing their financial papers and putting their final wishes in writing.

Whatever our beliefs about an afterlife may be, I think we can all agree on one thing: The only way we live on in *this* plane of reality is through the memories, thoughts, and feelings of those we leave behind. You have a clear choice about the way your spouse and family will forever remember you, at least when it comes to financial matters. You can leave them well taken care of, with a thoughtfully and clearly organized estate, or you can leave them with a scattered pile of loose ends and unresolved issues that lead to confusion, anger, embarrassment, debt, and/or family infighting.

The time to start building a positive legacy is now. Because the moment *will* come when it is too late to do anything about it. Benign neglect can be just as damaging as hostile action to the heirs you leave behind.

What Were They Thinking?

When we saddle our loved ones with our financial messes, they are left to wonder what we could possibly have been thinking. It seems such a careless and unloving thing to do. In the majority of cases, it is not lack of love that causes people to be irresponsible about final planning, but simple denial and avoidance.

We put off getting our final house in order for many of the same reasons we procrastinate in making a financial plan. But there's an even deeper issue at play here: our fear of death. It's just not a topic we want to think about. So we don't. We behave as if we're going to live forever. There's no urgency to do this paperwork *today*, we tell ourselves, because we're going to die *way* in the future. (Of course, the imagined "D" date moves further away the older we get.) In addition, we fear the will-making process will be costly, and we have a hard time justifying the expense *now*, when we have so many other present-moment priorities.

Final planning also involves making tough decisions and having tough conversations. The thought of dividing up our estate—who gets what and why?—brings up all sorts of emotions we'd rather avoid. It's often the *unspoken* agendas within families that prevent us from taking action—the elephants in the room that no one wants to talk about, like, "I don't trust my son's wife with my money."

The situation is intensified when there are second and third marriages involved, or children with special needs. In many cases, people would rather die than try to assign a dollar value to their various family relationships. And so that's exactly what they do.

For many high-net-worth individuals, there's also a fear of loss of control. They know they should start distributing their estate while they're still alive, but when push comes to shove, they really don't like giving up control. Many wealthy parents also like to control their children through their purse strings. They use their money as a way to influence their kids' behavior, and they don't like ceding that control by giving away the money or nailing down a concrete will.

The Messes We Leave Behind

If people really thought about the *consequences* of leaving financial messes to their families, they would be horrified—and appropriately so.

The messes we leave behind fall into several categories:

Life-and-death issues. Typically, when people fail to create a current will, they fail to address critical life issues such as the guardianship of their minor children. We talked about this earlier. They also typically fail to create a living will or a "durable power of attorney for health care"—otherwise known as a "pull the plug" document. And so the family is left to guess whether they wish to be resuscitated in a medical emergency and whether there are specific medical treatments they wish to seek or avoid. This can add enormous stress to an already stressful situation.

Taxes. Many people spend a huge amount of energy trying to avoid income tax—almost to the point of fraudulent behavior—yet, oddly enough, pay very little attention to the federal estate tax. For many wealthy people, this will be the largest single tax their family will ever pay. As of this writing, the exemptions are high—$5.43 million per person, meaning, a couple can transfer about $11 million to the next generation, tax-free—but these exemptions can, and probably *will*, change in the future. There are steps that can be taken to dramatically reduce the tax burden for your heirs, but unless you start taking those actions now, a huge portion of your estate may end up going to the IRS.

Privacy and control. If you don't get your basic house in order before you die, your estate is no longer private. It will need to be probated after your death. That means, the court steps in and says, "You didn't write anything down, so *we* have to sort through the mess and decide who gets what." That whole process is public, meaning that everything you own—all of your assets, including those of your business(es)—becomes public knowledge. This can be a source of embarrassment and harassment to your family. Probate is expensive, too, thanks to probate fees and attorneys' fees. It chips away at the value of your estate.

When you leave your estate in the hands of the government, you abandon choice. From a wealth-transfer perspective, there are only three potential recipients of your wealth: family members, charities, or the government. By setting up your estate intelligently and proactively, *you* get to decide who's first, second, and third on that list. By failing to plan, the government's plan becomes your default plan, and that's rarely a desirable situation.

Beneficiaries and trusts. Careless assignment of beneficiaries can cause enormous problems after your death. There are many assets, such as IRAs and life-insurance policies that transfer wealth without going through a will. They do this by assigning beneficiaries. Many people are surprisingly thoughtless and unconscious about who is named in these important documents. They may have filled out the papers at work thirty years ago and written down a name that made sense at the time, but no longer does. Sometimes beneficiary designations do not even coordinate with the estate plan; they're in conflict with the will and trust(s).

Major problems can also arise if you list a minor child, or a special-needs child, as a beneficiary. In most states, as soon as they reach the age of maturity, which is typically 18, they get full, unfettered access to that money.

If you have a trust in place, your assets may need to be re-titled in the name of that trust. If that hasn't been done, the trust may be meaningless. Also, there may be trustees, or beneficiaries, on the trust who are no longer alive or who no longer wish to serve. The trust might have been written at a time when the laws were vastly different from what they are today.

Bottom line: Any trust (or will) that's more than ten years old is probably obsolete or at least in need of a fresh look.

Family harmony. Probably the greatest type of wreckage that results from poor estate planning is family strife.

In the absence of a will, your family is often left in fear—fear that some strange uncle or cousin is going to crawl out of the woodwork and say, "I lent him $100,000, and he never paid me back." If you allow the government to settle your estate, then one family member might feel the ruling is unfair and decide to contest it. Now you have adversarial camps within the family, along with the possibility that attorneys and accountants will eat up all the money the government didn't take.

When you fail to make your wishes clearly known, you leave it up to your survivors to "do what you would have wanted"—which means you're trusting them to (1) know what your wishes are and (2) do the right thing. This is a huge leap of faith that is, sadly, unwarranted. One situation I've seen many times, for example, is a person who gets remarried and has children from a first marriage. Wanting to give the new spouse the proper respect (and wanting to avoid sleeping in the den forever), the person makes the new spouse the principal beneficiary in the will, saying, in effect, "I trust you to give my kids an equal share of the pie when I die."

But, of course, there's no guarantee that will happen. They're not the spouse's children, after all, so they might never see a dime. Or they may have to wait until the new spouse dies in order to get anything—and if the spouse is much younger than the deceased, that could mean waiting years or decades. Meanwhile, the estate slowly drains away as the spouse enjoys equestrian lessons and trips to Europe.

Very often problems occur simply because the deceased did not update the will to reflect his/her current wishes. For example, one child might have been out of favor twenty years ago and was cut out of the estate. Since that time, amends have been made, but the parent has failed to update the will. The other siblings *might* decide to remedy this imbalance, but . . . they might not.

Cleaning up the Mess

I'm convinced that if we were to spend ten solid minutes thinking about our own demise and its effect on our families—rather than shrinking away from the topic in discomfort—most of us would be motivated to take action.

Here are some areas you'll want to think about when you're ready to start cleaning up your messes and creating a positive legacy instead:

Start with the Basics

The very first thing you should put in place is the minimum package for estate planning. This includes a will, a power of attorney (POA), and a durable power of attorney (DPOA) for health care.

The will, of course, specifies your final wishes regarding your possessions and your dependents. It names your beneficiaries and also an *executor*, the person who will be in charge of ensuring that your stated desires are carried out. The POA names a person or persons whom you legally authorize to carry out certain actions on your behalf if you are unavailable to do so—things like signing checks or tax returns, or helping with a one-time event, such as the sale of a house. The power of attorney becomes inactive once the actions have been carried out or if you die or become incapacitated. The *durable* (hence the name) power of attorney kicks in when you become incapacitated. It allows a designated person to make critical decisions about your health care when and if you are unable to do so.

You can go on LegalZoom.com and get all these documents if you don't want to use an attorney.

Two more basic steps you'll want to take are listing of all your assets on one spreadsheet, as we talked about earlier, and creating a list of people your loved ones can call if they need more information about any aspect of your finances.

Trusts

As a general rule, if you want as much money as possible to go to your children, unfettered of taxes, the primary thing you need to do is to give up ownership while you're still in your oxygen-breathing years. You can't own it when you die. This is why people transfer assets into *trusts*. A trust is like a corporation; it exists independently of the individual(s).

A trust is a basically a bucket that holds money for the benefit of others over a long period of time. In the absence of a trust, a will transfers your property to the children outright. *With* a trust, you can leave the money in the "bucket," and the trust dictates the terms of payment over their lifetime. You are the one who sets the terms, so you, in effect, remain the puppet master, even after your death.

A trust is vitally important in the case of special-needs children, children with alcohol or drug problems, and children with disabilities who might require lifelong care. Giving these children a lump sum could be disastrous.

Life Insurance

One thing you might not realize is that the value of all your life-insurance death benefits counts as part of your overall estate.

That value can add up fast for high-net-worth people. If you have three $1 million policies, for example, you have now "used up" more than half of your $5.43 million exemption, and taxes will be due on more of your estate than you may have thought.

So individuals whose total estate comes near the exemption limit generally should never own their life insurance outright. Rather, it should be owned by a so-called insurance trust. This is a third-party entity that removes the death benefits from your federal estate tax. That's a low-hanging-fruit type of step you should take as you're doing your estate planning.

Beneficiaries

Thoughtful use of beneficiaries can be a great adjunct to traditional estate planning. If you name someone as a beneficiary on a life insurance policy or IRA, that person *will* receive that money, whether he or she is named in the will or not. Make sure you do a safety review of all your documents that have named beneficiaries.

If you want to name your children as beneficiaries, but they're still young, be careful about whom you name to act in their care. Many people name their parents or grandparents, but remember, those people may soon die or become too elderly to carry out their duties. Even if they don't, they have no legal obligation to give the money to the kids. And so you might be unintentionally disinheriting your children.

There are some creative things you can do through beneficiary designations to avoid that. For example, with life insurance, you can leave the money on deposit with the insurance company to be paid out over children's lifetime. That way, the kids get many bites of the apple, rather than an apple so large they'll choke on it.

Taxes

Again, estate taxes can be the largest tax your family ever pays. Estate tax is too complex a subject to cover in a few paragraphs, but the bottom line is that there are many excellent strategies you can use for reducing your family's tax burden. The key is to get some good advice and to take action early—i.e., *before* you're on your deathbed.

Thoughtless handling of assets within couples, for example, can cost your heirs millions of dollars. Remember: Every individual can bequeath $5.43 million (as of this writing) before estate taxes kick in. That's around $11 million for a couple. Also remember: A married couple can transfer unlimited wealth between the partners with no taxation. Married people often transfer their wealth to each other unthinkingly, causing them to lose one of their exemptions.

This situation can be avoided by using trusts.

Let's say you and I are a couple with a $20 million estate—that means $11 million can be left to our heirs free of federal estate tax; $9 million cannot. When I die, I might automatically transfer my half of our estate to you. Then, when you die, you might give it all to the children. What happens in this case is that I forfeit my $5.5 million exemption, because when you die, you can only use your single personal exemption of $5.5 million. Taxes will now need to be paid on $14.5 million.

But, if I take my $5.5 million and put it in a *trust* to the kids, that preserves both of our exemptions. The trust can pay you income for life, then, when you die, it can go to the children. What we've done here is create two buckets. Upon my death, my $5.5 million goes to the kids in a trust, tax-free. The rest of the estate—the other $14.5 million—goes to you, my spouse. Upon *your* death, you now get to claim *your* $5.5 million exemption. So, in the end, estate taxes need be paid on only $9 million, instead of $14.5 million. Huge difference—millions of dollars.

That's just one example of why you need to work on this now. A good advisor will offer several tax strategies aimed at your particular situation and goals.

Gifting

Many people are under the illusion that the way to avoid estate taxes is to gift the money away while you're alive. Well, the government isn't (completely) stupid. It has designed a parallel gift-tax system, which allows you to give away only a certain amount tax-free in your lifetime. Care to guess what that amount is? Yes, $5.43 million. So it doesn't matter whether you give it away now or later.

One good idea, if you want to start gifting your estate to your heirs now, is to take advantage of your *annual gift exclusion*. Both you and your spouse are allowed to gift a certain amount every year to each of your children, siblings, and grandchildren without affecting your lifetime exemption. As of this writing, that amount is $14,000, or 28,000 for a couple. So you can start giving away $28,000 a year to each of your heirs, tax-free, and still preserve your $5.43 million exemption. The earlier you start doing this, obviously, the more you can give away, penalty-free.

There are reasons that outright gifting may not be the best option. Simple example: You own a building you bought for $100,000, which is now worth $1 million. If you gift it to your children while you're alive, they will owe capital gains tax on its $900,000 appreciation when they go to sell it. If you leave it to them as an inheritance, however, the value is "stepped up" to its current value at the time of your death. When they go to sell it, they won't owe any taxes on the appreciation it earned before they inherited it.

Those are just a few ideas to get you thinking—not an exhaustive list, by any means. Everyone's situation is different and calls for different strategies and actions. The point is to start working sooner, rather than later, on estate planning. Timely action can make a world of difference to your loved ones.

Not a One-Time Step

I'd love to tell you that estate planning is a "do-it-and-forget-it" thing, but that's not the case. It's a dynamic and evolving process. Your thoughts about wealth transfer—how much to give the kids, how much to leave to charity—will probably change many times over the course of your lifetime. Your relationships with your heirs may change, too. Heirs may marry and remarry, have kids, go through personal crises. Some children may need more help than others.

Your financial condition also changes and evolves. A strategy that made sense when you had only $400,000 may no longer work when your estate is worth $10 million.

And, of course, laws change too. You and your advisor might have designed a plan that worked perfectly in conjunction with the tax laws that existed twenty-five years ago, but now there are new laws.

The point is that you want a plan that is flexible, and you want to revisit it often—at least every ten years, but ideally, more often than that. The more often you revisit your final plans, the more they become an integral part of your present thinking and behavior. And what you may find is that the fear and dread disappear, and are replaced by something new: peace of mind.

Peace of mind is the real and lasting benefit of good estate planning.

Knowing that you have a guardian for your minor children, a capable executor for your estate, and a clear plan that your family understands and is on board with can work wonders for your enjoyment of life in the here and now.

There is no reason to avoid working on your legacy. I like to tell my successful clients, "If you build your legacy with the same gusto and foresight with which you built your business, you can do some amazing things." Some of my clients, for example, create family foundations. These can be used to preserve and advance the values of the family—such as helping needy children or protecting endangered species. The children and grandchildren can serve on the board, where they become responsible for proposing meaningful ways to give the money away. This helps build character and trains the heirs to see financial stewardship as a tool for creating value in the world.

Many people fear that leaving their kids money—and *telling* the kids they're going to get money—will ruin their character. I don't agree. Money in itself does not affect character. There are people of good and bad character in both poor and wealthy families. I do believe, though, that including the children in your final planning (while maintaining some privacy about the details) gives you the opportunity to talk to them about financial stewardship and prepare them for the challenges and opportunities that lie ahead. Simply dumping a pile of money on people who may be unprepared for it, however, can be a setup for disaster.

Good final planning, ultimately, is an act of love.

Parting Thoughts

Did you recognize yourself in any of these chapters? *Some* of the chapters? *All* of the chapters? If so, don't be alarmed. Money mistakes can happen, but it usually means you're operating on bad information. The problem comes down to that age-old human dilemma: We don't know what we don't know. There are many aspects of personal finance that the average person *believes* he or she understands well enough to make sound decisions, but really doesn't. And it's those critical missing pieces that can make all the difference in the world.

I hope this book has helped in some small way to fill in the gaps in your own financial knowledge. I have tried to keep it simple, trusting that if any of the ideas grabs your attention, you will go out and do some more research on your own. This book was intended only to lay some basic groundwork and highlight some of the best financial strategies available (while exposing some of the costliest errors people commit). One book can't possibly cover everything.

Neither can any course, DVD, or combination of the above. That is why—as self-interested as it sounds—I strongly recommend sitting down with a qualified and experienced advisor. The world of finance is complicated. Investments, taxes, insurance, retirement planning, asset allocation: All of these areas can be studied for years. You probably don't have time to acquire in-depth knowledge on these topics and how they relate to one another. Why would you? You are too busy acquiring expertise in your own field. That's why it makes sense to sit down with someone who *does* have sufficient breadth and depth of knowledge in finance to help you design an intelligent, risk-adjusted plan that is perfectly suited to your unique situation.

Very few of us would try to learn how to play the cello, ride a horse, drive a tractor-trailer, fix a computer, or fly a plane without taking lessons from an expert. But when it comes to personal finances—a topic more complicated and life-affecting than any of these things—many of us insist upon going it alone. We pretend that the complex is elementary and forge blindly ahead.

I am not suggesting that the *handling* of your finances ought to be complicated. Not at all. In fact, if you're doing it right, it should be pretty simple. But again, that's why talking to an advisor helps. It's the *advisor's* job to sift through the complexities, to look at all the factors you are not trained to see, and to help you come up with a clear, actionable plan that you can stick to. And when you have questions about the bigger picture, you can pick up the phone and call the advisor. You have someplace to turn. A good advisor acts as your financial eyes and ears, your accountability partner, your information clearinghouse, and your coach.

But whether you work with an advisor or not, it's time to start putting together a plan that works. Take a look at the planning pyramid and apply it to your situation. Review your risk-management vehicles. Start keeping track of your assets from month to month. Get rolling on your 401(k) or other retirement plan. Write down your goals and ask yourself how you plan to achieve them. Look at your assets in terms of your three buckets—immediate needs, 3–7-year needs, and 7-plus-year needs. Are you taking too much risk? Are you taking enough?

Planning for the future can seem like an unwelcome distraction. After all, there are always more pressing financial needs in the present moment—when to replace the roof, how to pay this year's tuition, when to trade in the car. But what I urge you to realize is that planning for the future *pays immediate dividends in the here and now.* The moment you come clean about your money reality and put together a working plan for the future, you begin to notice the kinds of life changes my clients report seeing. Stress and anxiety go down. Guilt and worry ease. You start to sleep with greater peace of mind. You gain a compass for making money decisions, large and small. You find yourself able to plan future events, such as weddings, with joy and confidence. Optimism and hope increase. This leads to feelings of greater overall happiness and resilience, which affects every aspect of your life, from your career to your relationships to the pursuit of your dreams.

Working toward a brighter financial future translates immediately into a more fulfilling present.

And you can't put a price tag on that.